SHIPWRECK & SURVIVAL IN OMAN, 1763

KLAAS DOORNBOS

Shipwreck & Survival in Oman, 1763

The Fate of the Amstelveen *and Thirty Castaways on the South Coast of Arabia*

Based on the Notes of Cornelis Eyks

AMSTERDAM UNIVERSITY PRESS

Dedicated to Cornelis Eyks,
a seaman who knew how to write

An earlier edition of this book has been published in 2012
[ISBN 978 90 8555 059 4]

Translation: Vertaalbureau Scandinavia, The Hague
Editing: Vivien Collingwood, Heemstede

Cover illustration: Sybren de Graaff, *Desert Arabian Peninsula*, 1996
Cover and lay-out: Sander Pinkse Boekproductie, Amsterdam

ISBN   978 90 8964 838 9
e-ISBN 978 90 4852 688 8
NUR   685

Preface

In years gone by, Dutch East Indiamen journeying to the Persian Gulf would often first sail to Muscat to take in fresh drinking water, to purchase fish, fruit and other provisions, and to conduct trade. In 1763, however, one of these ships — the *Amstelveen* — came to grief: she ran aground at night on the south coast of the Arabian Peninsula, and was shattered in the heavy surf. The accident always remained a mystery. This changed recently, with the discovery of the *Notes* written by Cornelis Eyks, a ship's mate who survived the shipwreck. The circumstances of the disaster became clearer, and more could be found out about the castaways' gruelling trek along the hot desert coast. The events that occurred almost unnoticed in Oman at that time are retold, explained and examined here, with the help of Eyks' logbook and data from the archives.

Eyks describes how the Bedouin and the people living on the coast reacted to the passing strangers. At the same time, he gives us an impression of local maritime trade and the role played by European maritime powers in the Gulf. Those on the remote south coast had little knowledge of such things. Only once when the men reached Al Hadd were they recognised: '*Portugees! Englees! Hollandees!*'

Writing a book in another field demands quite a bit of studying, and, occasionally, very concrete help. Time and again I found what I was looking for in meticulously edited maritime historical studies, and in the archives, I was often provided with more than I had needed. I am grateful to many people for their hints, advice and warnings. Many a tribute can be found in the list of consulted literature. The list also contains news reports and articles that I was able to track down at an early stage, thanks to tips from Guus Lindeman and Ben Slot, both of whom had previously published on the shipwreck of the *Amstelveen*.

I think back with great pleasure on the collaboration with Diederick Kortlang of the Dutch National Archives. With his assistance, and thanks to the digitisation of parts of the VOC archives, it was possible to reconstruct the muster roll of the *Amstelveen*'s final intra-Asiatic journey in just a few weeks.

I was very fortunate to gain the full support of the Dutch ambassador in Oman, H.E. Stefan van Wersch. His enthusiasm was the key factor in inspiring local interest in Eyks' story.

At the opening of the splendid exhibition on Oman in Amsterdam's *Nieuwe Kerk* in 2009, I met H.E. Mohammad Al Zubair, founder of the *Bait Al Zubair Museum* in Muscat. On the basis of what he already had heard and my description of some other striking details of Eyks' trek, he spontaneously promised to arrange for a translation into Arabic as soon as the English text was ready. Translation into English was achieved thanks to two valiant translators and a very dedicated editor. Ideas concerning on-site research, a documentary and an exhibition were also given a warm reception.

To advance bilateral cooperation in respect of these projects, on 2 May 2011 in Muscat, a Memorandum of Understanding was signed between the Sultanate of Oman and the Kingdom of the Netherlands. In 2013, a conference and an exhibition will be held in remembrance of the loss of the *Amstelveen* 250 years ago. A modest plaque on Cape Mataraca will commemorate the disaster and, at the same time, mark the starting point of the castaways' trek to Muscat.

There are no old pictures of the south coast of Oman. Thanks to Wiekert Visser I was able to fill this gap with some nice photographs of the Sharqiyah coast.

Finally, a word of thanks and appreciation for Gert-Jan Keizer, the art dealer who found Eyks' logbook. His happy find did not lead to the digging up of a long-lost treasure, but his keen interest in the shipwreck and the historical trek has been a lasting stimulus to me, writing this book. Thanks to his generosity, Eyks' story will not quickly sink into obscurity again.

K.D.

Contents

Prologue   9
The VOC at home and in Asia   13
A mysterious accident   18
The Dutch East Indiaman *Amstelveen*   21
In the Bay of Sawqirah   34
Two old letters   44
At Cape Mataraca (Ras Madrakah)   49
Forsaken in the desert   55
Along the Gulf of Masirah   59
Hunger, thirst, rocks and robbers   61
Trapped by the Bedouin   65
At a forked river (near Duqm)   66
Saved by some water   69
The fate of the little Javanese boy   72
A warmer welcome   75
Through the high sand dunes   79
Encounters on the Sharqiyah coast   83
A cunning merchant captain in Hadd   89
Arrival in Muscat   92
Unrest in the Arabian merchant fleet   97
With the Resident on Kharg   101
Salt from Bandar Abbasi   104
A surprising reunion in Muscat   106
To Batavia by way of Cochin   110
To Muscat once again   114
Back in Middelburg at last   117
Cornelis Eyks, a life at sea   122
Causes and location of the disaster   129
Those on board and their fate   133
Remaining mysteries   138
'The salvaged people'   141
Acknowledgments   143
Bibliography   145

1 – *Muscat in Arabia.* Old city view of Muscat, with two Dutch East Indiamen anchored in the roadstead and several smaller vessels moored in the bay. Engraving, Jan Jansz. Struys, Amsterdam, 1676.

Prologue

Some years ago, in the summer of 1997, one of my friends came across an 18th-century book in an antiques market in southern France: a collection of stories in Dutch. He casually glanced through it. His attention was caught by the word 'Amstelveen' in the title of one of the stories. Interesting, he thought, that's where I live; and he bought the book without much further thought. Only when he got home did he realise that the story was not about the place where he lived, but about the stranding of a ship, the *Amstelveen*, an East Indiaman belonging to the Dutch East India Company (VOC). This was perhaps even more interesting, but he did little more about it until the middle of 2008, when another resident of Amstelveen suddenly published an article on the Internet entitled '*The VOC ships Amstelland and Amstelveen*'. The article mentioned a failed attempt to dive to the wreck of the *Amstelveen* in the 1990s. No reference was made to the old book, and nothing was to be found relating to the book's author, Cornelis Eyks from Middelburg, third mate on the *Amstelveen*.

In the autumn of 2008, he asked me to work out, on the basis of Eyks' narrative, where the ship had been wrecked: 'Where is the wreck and what might be left of it? Might it still be possible to salvage something of the cargo?' It is hard to conceive of a more fascinating puzzle for someone who, since the age of twelve, had sailed on the Wadden Sea for more than fifty summers, and who has also sailed rather a lot elsewhere. Even across the Indian Ocean, from Malacca to Djibouti, but obviously far from the coast of the Arabian Peninsula — as one would expect.

The mystery of the shipwreck in calm weather, on a coast that had been navigated frequently since time immemorial, initially appeared relatively straightforward. Eyks had apparently painstakingly recorded the navigational data from the ship's logbook for the day on which the *Amstelveen* had been lost. After a few weeks, I thought that I could identify the location; but because I was not entirely sure of my conclusion, I hesitated to commit myself. I told the owner where, in my opinion, the accident had most likely occurred; the place where remains or traces of the wreck might be found. With a touch of sadness, I gave the book back. Perhaps it had suddenly become a very valuable book. After all, who has never dreamed — after a languid, windless day on the water — of a rich cargo in an age-old shipwreck?

Eyks' logbook covers a period of three years. Thirty members of the crew survived the shipwreck. The story of their journey on foot through the desert

2 – The village of Amstelveen about 1780. In late 18th century Amstelveen was a quiet rural municipality with 5000 inhabitants, mainly farmers and peat cutters, living in and around a small village also called Amstelveen, just south of Amsterdam. Several rich citizens of that city built their country houses in this neighbouring arcadia. Investing in another new ship on behalf of the VOC Chamber of Amsterdam, some of these wealthy citizens named this ship *Amstelveen* as a tribute to their beloved country place. Those days are gone. Now Amstelveen is a modern city with 80.000 inhabitants, stuck between Amsterdam and Schiphol Airport, but for commuters still a nice residential nucleus. Drawing by J. Bulthuis (1750–1801).

along the south coast of Oman continued to haunt me. Would it be possible to transform that part of the account into a gripping book — perhaps a film script — without revealing the ultimate secret?

Of course, one cannot simply publish information about the location of an old wreck just like that. In 1992, this had been the reason for concealing the location of the dive to try to find some remains of the wreck of the *Amstelveen*. A short time before, the wreck of her sister ship, the *Geldermalsen*, had been discovered in the shallow waters east of Sumatra and plundered. In 1986, the auction of the cargo of gold and porcelain had yielded around 37 million guilders.

The data in the archives, however, showed that the *Amstelveen* had carried mainly sugar and spices, and there could be little or nothing left of the wreck. I was given the opportunity to go ahead, and this book is the result of that endeavour.

In his *Notes*, Eyks gave a moving account of the shipwreck and, without realising it, a historically interesting account of a weeks-long wander through the southern Arabian desert. A true survival trek to the civilised world, undertaken by a band of destitute, desperate sailors, walking barefoot over countless steep cliffs, exhausted by hunger and thirst, robbed time and again, trekking virtually naked across red-hot desert sand dunes and seemingly endless beaches, and begging for food and water from people living on the coast, who gradually began to respond in a friendlier and more hospitable way.

Nothing was to be found about Eyks' logbook, but a few things were known about the fate of the crew and the cargo of the unfortunate ship. Moreover, this information came from just one source: a letter of 1763, kept in the VOC archives in The Hague. The location of the accident was stated briefly in the letter. The ship and her cargo had been lost in their entirety at Cape Mataraca. The great majority of the people on board, including the captain and all but one of the officers, had perished.

In 1992, the *Amstelveen* suddenly made the headlines again as a result of the divers' plans. In 1993, another article was published by Frits Huis, '*Martelgang naar Muscat*' [An agonising journey to Muscat]; and that was it. The naval disaster, which had already been forgotten in the 18th century, sunk once more into obscurity. Nor did anyone remember Cornelis Eyks, third mate on the *Amstelveen* and leader of the surviving seamen; not even in Zeeland, where he was born, in Middelburg.

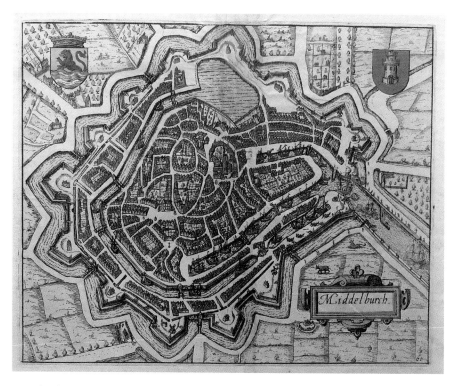

3 – A bird's eye view of Middelburg about 1640: the harbour, the VOC shipyard and a part of the city's canal to the Westerschelde. Upper left the provincial coat of arms of Zeeland *Luctor et Emergo*, to the opposite the municipal arms of Middelburg.

The diver who had searched for the wreck turned out to be a fellow country-man working in Oman, but 'the location was — very understandably, due to the possibility of thieves — not named.'[1] While it was possible to discover the location, it did not correspond to the general indication in the old letter to the Governor-General in Batavia, nor to what Eyks had noted in his logbook.

Where could the men have begun their trek, and how far did they have to walk in order to reach the civilised world again? Did the story of their wandering journey indeed tally with the location of the wreck that I had thought plausible after my first analysis? Would it ever be possible to definitively solve the riddle of the location? Piece by piece, these questions are addressed in this book.

The main objective, however, is to finally give recognition to the ordeal that was undergone by the surviving seamen, who wandered through that deathly silent, barren, stone-dry, hellishly-hot wilderness, with its merciless bandits and overly curious fishermen. The spectre of the threatening and thieving Bedouin would doubtless have stayed with the seamen their whole lives. But no one was murdered on the way! That was cause for amazement, especially in Muscat. Closer to Hadd, they gradually received more help from hospitable people: benevolent fishermen and generous, sympathetic women. This was their salvation, and those who made it to safety would doubtless have often looked back on this with gratitude.

1 G. Lindeman, *De VOC-schepen Amstelland en Amstelveen* [The VOC ships Amstelland and Amstelveen]. In: *Het Profiel* [The Profile], Afd. Amsterdam e.o. AWN, June 2008. I used Google Earth to help discover the location.

The voc at home and in Asia

On Friday, 5 August 1763, a fine Dutch East Indiaman named *Amstelveen* ran aground on the immense south coast of the Arabian Peninsula. The *Amstelveen* was a huge regular cargo vessel owned by the Dutch East India Company, sailing from Batavia (Jakarta, Indonesia) to Kareek (Kharg) in the Persian Gulf.

The *'United East India Company'* — in Dutch, the *'Verenigde Oost-Indische Compagnie'* (voc) — was formed in 1602 as a trading company with a monopoly on shipping east of the Cape of Good Hope. Other Dutch shipping companies were no longer permitted to take part in the lucrative, but rather risky,

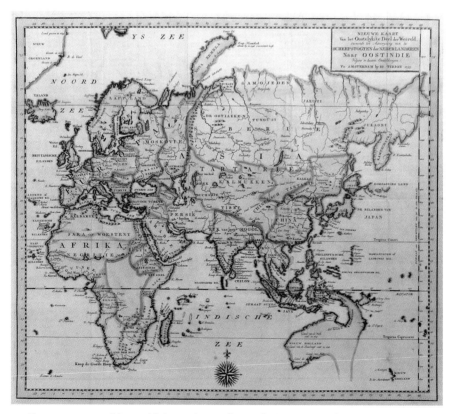

4 – *The eastern part of the world.* A popular small map depicting Australia still as *New Holland.* East of the Cape of Good Hope the voc has been active in international trade and warfare, mainly against fortresses and ships of Portugal and Spain. Is. Tirion, Amsterdam, 1753.

5 – Amsterdam, the City Hall (Royal Palace since 1815) and the Nieuwe Kerk (left) on the Dam. Engraved optical view by Daumont, Paris, 1760.

6 – The city and harbour of Amsterdam in an early 18th century overview with the municipal arms proudly in the front and a caption in Latin and German referring to the most principal buildings of the then prosperous metropolis. Engraving by J.F. Leizel after F.B. Werner, Augsburg, M. Engelbrecht, ±1730.

7 – The VOC shipyard at Middelburg. Caption in Dutch and French besides the monogram of the VOC Chamber of Zealand (Z) in Middelburg (M). Optical view, J.B. Probst, Augsburg 1778.

merchant voyages to the East Indies. The VOC, established in Amsterdam, was in fact a conglomerate of shipping companies. The Company was firmly rooted in six cities, already prosperous seaports[2] in Holland and Zeeland, the most influential provinces of the Republic of the Seven United Provinces. At first, the aim of the new Company was to secure a regular and profitable supply of spices from the Malay Archipelago. Soon afterwards, the Company expanded to import tea and porcelain from China, pepper and textiles from India, cinnamon from Ceylon, coffee and sugar from Java, and many other goods. The business quickly developed into a powerful international concern that continued its large-scale activities in Asia until 1795.

The VOC was also an important source of prosperity at home, mainly in Holland and Zeeland. The building, equipping and stocking of the ships, and the sale (mainly by auction) of the imported goods, made the VOC the country's largest employer by far for nearly two centuries.

2 Amsterdam, Middelburg (Zeeland), Rotterdam, Delft, Enkhuizen and Hoorn, each town with an independent Chamber responsible for their ships and collectively for the Company as a whole.

The keel of the *Amstelveen* was laid in 1746 at the VOC shipyard in Amsterdam. In the 18th century, about six to eight East Indiamen were launched there every year. The *Amstelveen* was one of the largest cargo vessels built by the VOC. The Company also had a yard for the construction of such large ships in Middelburg, a small city on Walcheren Island in Zeeland with a canal connecting the harbour of Middelburg to the roadstead of Rammekens and the deep waters of the Scheldt.

In 1762, the *Amstelveen* sailed for the fifth time from the Netherlands to Batavia. Six months later, in June 1763, she was used on one of the VOC's many trade routes in Asia: that from Batavia to the Persian Gulf. All kinds of commodities were shipped along the Company's regular routes between its trading posts in Japan, China, Siam (Thailand) the Malay Archipelago, Malacca, Bengal, Coromandel, Ceylon, the Malabar Coast (the south-west coast of India), Suratte, Persia (Gamron, Bushehr) and the Arab world (Mocha, Muscat, Basra). Throughout Asia, money was earned to purchase spices, tea and other valuable goods for the return voyage to the Netherlands. In a nautical sense, the route to the Persian Gulf was a simple one. Nevertheless, the ships often took a long time to sail it, owing to a lack of wind and long delays at the ports where they were unloaded and loaded. They often had to wait for favourable monsoon winds as well.

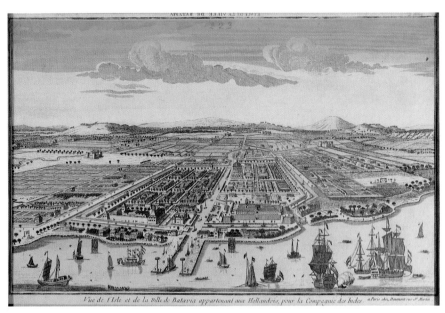

8 – Batavia on Java, several ships in the roadstead. In the centre of this bird's eye view the Casteel (the walled government buildings of the VOC) with many warehouses, accessible through a canal. Utmost right a gallows-lee, and in the distance the much healthier hilly regions. Engraving, Daumont, Paris, 1770.

After 1620, the entrepôt at Batavia grew to be the Company's administrative centre in Asia. It was the seat of the Governor General who, together with the Governing Council of the VOC, was the Company's highest representative in Asia. The so-called High Government in Batavia was the VOC's supreme executive power in Asia, responsible for trade and diplomacy, military action and jurisdiction. Batavia was also the logistic centre of the VOC with many warehouses, a hospital and a shipyard for the maintenance of the ships. The Company as a whole was run from the Netherlands by the VOC's highest board of administrators, *the Heren XVII* (Lords Seventeen) in Amsterdam.

A mysterious accident

The VOC had thus been active in Asia for 160 years when the *Amstelveen* was lost. This stately sailing vessel departed on 16 June 1763 from the roadstead of Batavia with 105 persons on board and a cargo of sugar, tin and spices. Her destination was Kareek, a small island in the Persian Gulf near Basra. The VOC had bought Kharg in 1753 from a local Persian ruler and set up a walled trading post there: Fort Mosselstein, named after Jacob Mossel, then Governor General in Batavia. Fort Mosselstein was administrated by an experienced merchant bearing the title of Resident, and used for the storage and sale of all kinds of merchandise.

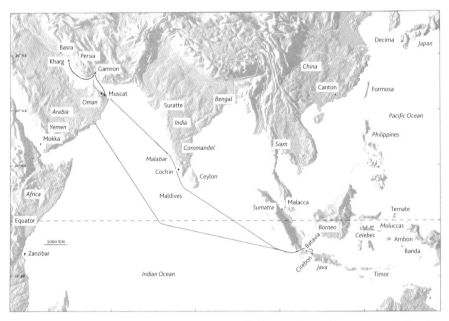

9 – The trade area of the VOC in Asia, the voyage of the *Amstelveen* from Java to the Persian Gulf and the return trip of Eyks from Kharg via Gamron, Muscat and Cochin to Batavia. According to the printed VOC sailing directions the *Amstelveen* sailed under the equator through the Equatorial Channel (the passage between both groups of the Maldiven Islands) and then in a NW direction towards the south coast of Oman.

The voyage of the *Amstelveen* across the Indian Ocean and the Arabian Sea initially went well, but ended in disaster on the Arabian coast. One evening, the ship suddenly ran aground in slightly foggy weather, and fell prey to unprecedentedly high waves rising from behind. It fell apart in the breakers near a low, deserted beach.

Only 30 of those on board succeeded in reaching the coast on pieces of wreckage. The cause of the shipwreck has remained a mystery. Judging by his chart and dead reckoning, the captain had chosen a safe course. A lookout had been kept all day long from the topmast, but no one had seen land ahead. Things nevertheless went desperately wrong during a short, nearly windless period, with disastrous consequences.

After a few months, perhaps several years, the last remains of the wooden hull had disappeared in the breakers or had been washed ashore. Any valuable items had been picked up and sold or reused. In the course of time, almost nobody could remember where the great ship had gone down. It never became really clear how the strange accident could have happened. Did she end up in fatal circumstances due to severe negligence, as concluded in Batavia after some survivors were questioned, and set out in a High Government Resolution of 15 June 1764? Or did the ship simply sail onto the coast, as presumed by Ben Slot (1993) in an interesting article about the accident? Or did something else happen? The ship had deviated a long way from her prescribed course, and had run aground in a place where VOC ships had no business and where they usually also did not go.

Until recently, the VOC's harsh judgments concerning the actions of the captain and first mate could not be verified, let alone convincingly refuted.

Cornelis Eyks from Middelburg was the only naval officer to survive the shipwreck. He, just like the others who had narrowly escaped drowning, embarked on an exhausting trek to the inhabited world. Eyks and his men walked to Ras Al Hadd, a striking cape in the extreme north-east of Oman; what would later prove to have been a journey of more than 500 km as the crow flies. Together with a few companions, he sailed from there on a local vessel via Sur to Matrah near Muscat; a further journey of more than 200 km. On 11 September 1763, they walked to Muscat, where they were received by the local VOC agent.

Eyks reported the loss of the *Amstelveen* three weeks later to Mr Buschman, Resident of the VOC in Fort Mosselstein on Kharg. The Resident sent Eyks to Batavia to be questioned about the accident. While under way, Eyks wrote his *Notes (Aantekeningen)*, a unique personal account of the shipwreck and his trek in the desert and along the coast of Oman. These *Notes* were published in 1766 in his native city of Middelburg, and then soon forgotten. In 1997, they were rediscovered in France. Eyks' logbook contained the necessary clues for the explanation and location of the shipwreck, and above all, an impressive account of a survival journey through a desert area twice as large as the Netherlands, where as far as is known no European previously passed through.[3]

To provide some background to Eyks' account of the shipwreck, I will first tell something of the ship and the coastal area along which it sailed and went down. We then follow Eyks' account of the shipwreck and the barren survival journey in the heat along the Sharqiyah coast of Oman. The events that occurred in the wake of the disaster are also fascinating: Eyks' welcome in Muscat, his voyage to Kharg with an Arabian merchant fleet and his dispatch to Batavia by way of Muscat and Cochin on the Malabar Coast (India). A year later, he returned to Muscat, and then sailed back to the Netherlands by way of Batavia and the Cape. In conclusion, a few words are offered on Eyks' life as a seaman, the underlying causes and most likely location of the shipwreck, the fate of those on board and a number of as yet unsolved mysteries that this new research into the loss of the *Amstelveen* has brought to light.

3 In the summer of 1792, thus 29 years after Eyks and his men, another much smaller group of American castaways walked about 160 km through this area, also barefooted. They continued the last part of their trek (from Masirah to Muscat) on camels guided by local people. Their experiences were reported by Daniel Saunders after his return in the US in 1794.

The Dutch East Indiaman Amstelveen

The *Amstelveen* was about 50 metres long — not counting the enormous bow-sprit — and almost 13 metres wide. The ship had a cargo capacity of 1,150 tons and was one of the largest ships sailing the oceans at the time. Old VOC cargo vessels spent their last sailing days in often-calm Asiatic waters, until it became too expensive to maintain them. In this way, the Dutch always had about 100–150 ships available in Asia, which were for the most part much larger than the Arabian and other Asiatic cargo vessels of the time.[4]

What did such ships actually look like, and how did they sail the high seas? Where was the *Amstelveen* going on this occasion? Who was on board and what was being transported on this voyage? Anyone who wants to understand how this mysterious accident happened needs to know detailed answers to such questions. After all, Dutch ships had sailed to Arabian and Persian ports for more than 140 years without any trouble. This was the only accident to befall a Dutch East Indiaman in that region.

Initially, Company ships sailed mainly to Mocha in the Red Sea and through the Gulf of Oman to Gamron (Bandar Abbas). They often anchored in the roadstead of Muscat.[5] In 1753, Fort Mosselstein on Kharg was built to promote trade in Basra and to better protect the Company against English expansionary ambitions in the Gulf. The VOC's posts in Bushir and Gamron were closed down. Muscat remained a favourite port of call for Dutch ships, however. There, they were not only able to stock up on water, fruit and other fresh food, but also to conduct trade with local merchants.

The VOC had an agent in Muscat, Naraitun,[6] probably an Indian merchant who spoke Dutch and acted as the local intermediary for the Company's trading activities. To the annoyance of the High Government in Batavia, however, he was also involved in the prohibited private trade by seamen from Dutch

---

4 This also entailed great risks. If a disaster occurred, there were often many victims, and cargos equal to those of several local vessels were lost all at once.

5 'Masqat' is the official Dutch spelling of Muscat. Usually, Eyks wrote Maskat. In the past, it was also written as Mascate, Maskate, Maskatte, Muskette, Musquette, Muschette and Musquetta.

6 Narriton, Naraitoen, Narrottam, Naraitun; the spelling varies. 'Naraitun' is perhaps the best way to write it. Buschman wrote Naraitoen; he himself probably wrote Naraitun.

Oostelyk gedeelte van AMSTERDAM, AMSTERDAM vers le point de l'Est,
van het Y te zien. presé du TY.

10 – Amsterdam, the eastern part of the harbour with an East Indiaman arriving, a dredging machine in the front and the VOC shipyard in the distance. Optical view with the city coat of arms, by G.M. Probst, ca 1770.

ships.[7] Eyks met him three times, and his logbook reveals in guarded terms what he secretly thought of Naraitun's dealings.

Unfortunately, there are no known illustrations of the *Amstelveen*. She was a homeward-bounder, built for the long voyage across the Atlantic and Indian Oceans to the East Indies and back. When loaded, she had a draw of six to seven metres: an impressive floating castle, armed on both sides with four heavy cannons. She was a seaworthy three-master with a long bowsprit and a sturdy wooden figurehead in front, and at the back, a high poop surrounded by the stern and an orlop deck for officers with full bladders. The distinguished character of the poop deck was enhanced by a beautifully worked stern at the back of the ship. What the decorative carving on the stern represented is unknown, but the coat of arms of the village of Amstelveen would certainly have been present. A VOC ship with a flat stern was called a 'square-sterned East Indiaman,' due to that strikingly high stern.

7 In a letter from the High Government in Batavia dd. 24 May 1764, Naraitun was told in no uncertain terms not to become involved in private trade by servants of the Company.

11 – An East Indiaman is a complex ocean-going sailing ship, repeatedly depicted and described in rare old folios and many modern books. This picture was taken from a famous early book: C. ALLARD, *Nieuwe Hollandse scheeps-bouw* (New Dutch ship-building), 1695. (Reprinted and enlarged in 1705, 1716, 1719 and 1739).

Around 1750, large square-sterned East Indiamen had two continuous decks across the full length of the hull and a quarterdeck behind the large mast.[8] In front of the large mast, on the low middle deck (the waist), a longboat was transported: a large boat for transporting water, provisions and cargo. Within the longboat was a small boat for conveying persons to and from the shore. In suitable weather, the small boat was also used on the high seas to carry crew members or passengers to other ships in the fleet. When a ship fell into distress, the longboat was used as a lifeboat to save pas-

12 – Municipal coat of arms of Amstelveen with four Andreas crosses.

8 It is possible to visit a splendid replica of such an East Indiaman: the AMSTERDAM. This ship is moored at the Maritime Museum (*Scheepvaartmuseum*) in the port of Amsterdam.

S'LANTS ZEE-MAGAZYN EN SCHEEPS TIMMERWERF

13 – The VOC shipyard of the Chamber of Amsterdam c. 1700. Nowadays, the large repository to the right provides accommodation for the city's Maritime Museum. Engraving by J. Mulder in C. Crommelin, reissued by Joh. Wagenaar, 1760.

sengers and prominent members of the crew.[9] There was certainly not enough room for everyone. In his logbook, Eyks described how events unfolded after the *Amstelveen* ran aground, when the longboat came to grief. All of the prominent members of the crew were drowned.

The construction of a square-sterned East Indiaman required at least 600 large, suitable oak trees. These were imported from Germany along the Rhine using timber rafts, and from Denmark and the Baltic countries by sea. Carefully chosen tree trunks were drenched in timber ponds with brackish water and sawn in mills that were driven by wind power. The construction of the ship's hull took six to eight months. After launching, the finishing and equipping took at least another six months. The new ship was then sailed across the shallow Zuiderzee to the roadstead of Texel. That is where most of the crew came on board, and only then was the ship ballasted: loaded with building materials for Batavia and outposts elsewhere in Asia, and with all kinds of articles for the main-

9 Survivors of the *Geldermalsen* were blamed for having done nothing to save the officers or 'the most virtuous crew who stayed on board with the captain' (C.J.A. Jörg, 1986, p. 48).

DE PUT, DIE WATER AAN DE SCHEPEN VERSCHAFT, OP TEXEL, HET SCHILD IN 'T VERSCHIET,

14 – 'The well providing water to the ships in the roadstead of Texel, in the distance the village of Oudeschild.' Excellent dune water was transported to Oudeschild and then transferred to the ships in a longboat. Engraving by T. de Roode after P. v. Kuyk, 1760, Delft, M. Roelofswaert, plm. 1770.

tenance of the ships, mainly at the shipyard on Onrust Island, near Batavia. In the Texel roadstead, casks of fresh water and provisions were also brought on board. The rest of the crew, soldiers and any passengers arrived from Den Helder just before departure. After the muster roll had been checked, the ship sailed as soon as the wind was favourable, at outgoing tide, via the Marsdiep on to the high seas: to the Cape of Good Hope and then on to the East Indies.

The maiden voyage[10] of the *Amstelveen* commenced on 27 October 1747, together with four other East Indiamen: the *Osdorp*, the *Slot van Kapelle*, the *Eindhoef* and the *Fortuin*. The *Vosmaar*, a brand-new ship built in the VOC shipyard in Middelburg under the authority of the Chamber of Zeeland, departed two days later from the roadstead of Rammekens, near Vlissingen. This ship probably joined the Texel fleet at the Heads near Dover, and on her, a young ordinary seaman named Cornelis Eyks was also sailing for the first time to the East Indies! Three such fleets departed every year, sometimes inter-

10 This first voyage from Amsterdam to Batavia ended in disaster. The *Amstelveen* arrived safe and sound, but under way an excessive number of people on board had died (over 80). Many sick people also remained behind at the Cape. On the *Slot van Kapelle*, proportionately even more people on board died (more than 130).

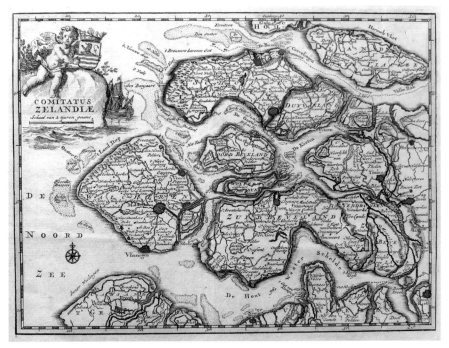

15 – The Province of Zeeland with the Scheldt, Flushing (Vlissingen) and the canal from the roadstead of Rammekens to Middelburg.

spersed by a single ship: often a smaller vessel sailing on its own.

Ships like the *Amstelveen* usually made five to seven return voyages to the East Indies. After each voyage, they were cleaned and checked for seaworthiness. A report was made on their condition for the local equipment master. Among other things, such reports served as guidelines for repair work, for which this high-ranking official was responsible. This enabled the ships to sail for about fifteen to twenty years in demanding conditions, before the cost of maintenance became too high. Old ships, however, were usually sold, laid up or scrapped after they had been used for another few years for merchant shipping in the Indian Archipelago and other calm routes in Asian waters. The age of the *Amstelveen* may well have been taken into consideration when it was decided to use her for a voyage to the Gulf. She was, after all, already sixteen years old and certainly no longer in impeccable condition, as would quickly become apparent.

At sea, watch seems to have been kept in the customary way: twice a day, four hours on, eight hours off. Four hours of work were followed by a period of eight free hours for rest, meals and the like. This held for both the officers and the sailors with deck duty. During a four-hour watch, the 'duty officer' — the captain, the first mate or the second mate — was in command, assisted by a third mate. According to a fixed schedule, after the watch ended, both officers in charge were relieved by two others who had just had eight hours of rest.

During the fifth outward voyage of the Amstelveen, there was no second mate on board either. There was a first mate, who fell ill under way and died in hospital shortly after arriving in Batavia. The lack of a second mate must have compelled Captain Pietersen to adjust the duty roster when the ship was still in the Texel roadstead. The first mate's illness shortly after departure from the Cape meant that the duty roster had to be changed again, but how this was done is not known. On the way from Batavia to Kharg, practically the same situation occurred with a new crew commanded by the same captain. Eyks subsequently wrote to Buschman that during the disaster, the captain, first mate and two old navigators had drowned. Again, there was no second mate on board. Most likely, there was no qualified first mate either, but there was an additional third mate. Eyks did not mention him. His presence on board was revealed in the VOC Archive (inv.no. 6415).

On the *Amstelveen*, the captain was on duty with a third mate in the early morning, from 4 a.m. to 8 a.m., and in the afternoon and early evening, from 4 p.m. to 8 p.m. The first mate was on duty from 8 a.m. to 12 noon, and during the first part of the night, from 8 p.m. to 12 midnight. According to his logbook, Eyks was present at the transfer of the evening watch to the first mate. As third mate, he was charged with following the latter's instructions and commands. It is not entirely clear how this was arranged during the graveyard watch between midnight and 4 a.m., and during the afternoon watch from 12 noon to 4 p.m. There was no second mate on board.

A surgeon, a chaplain and a military commander were also among the officers. The petty officers included a boatswain, a sail maker, a second boatswain, a cook, and a surgeon's first and second mate. Naturally, many seamen were needed on such a big, demanding ship. They were appointed in ranks — junior seaman, ordinary seaman, sailor, and so on — according to experience, with corresponding differences in pay. The seamen did the most difficult and dangerous work at sea. They were available day and night when needed. In normal circumstances, however, they were active during the day, and at least some of them were also on duty during one of the two night watches. For this purpose, they were divided into shifts (*bakken*).[11] Their domain was the front half of the

---

11 A shift work system was used on board. A shift ('*bak*') was led by the boatswain or boatswain's mate. The boatswain's mate did the same job, but was responsible for work in and around the foremast. Each shift ate together. The food was picked up in a large wooden mess trap (*bak*), from which each ladled his portion. The word *bak* (for 'shift') stems from this practice.

ship. They did the dirty work, lived at close quarters on and under the forecastle deck, and slept without privacy in stuffy, stale areas. Experienced seamen who could also operate naval cannons were called ship's gunners (*bosschieters*). In severe weather and other dangerous situations — storms, pirates, fire — the order for everyone was 'all hands!' For the lowest in rank, this often meant having to spend many hours pumping, often without knowing what was happening around them. But everyone knew what was at stake: sink or swim.

The captain, mates, surgeon, master gunner (a military officer) and passengers, if any, had separate cabins in the stern. In the daytime, they usually stayed on the poop deck and also ate there together. The relaxed atmosphere and copious meals on voyages to the East and back to the Netherlands[12] were in sharp contrast to the often rough sailor's life and the rather monotonous meals from the mess, eaten by crew members on the fore part of the ship.

On board, the time was announced by the careful ringing of the ship's bell. During the watch, each half-hour was marked by one more stroke than the time before. Eight strokes — consisting of four groups of two strokes, rung in close succession — marked the change of the watch. An even number of strokes indicated one of the whole hours during that watch. Two strokes during the afternoon watch thus meant that it was 1 p.m. At night, the bell was not rung with the clapper but by tapping a knife against the ship's bell. It could be heard easily on the poop, but it did not bother those sleeping in the stern.

Inches, feet and fathoms (1.88 m) were used for linear measurements. Distances were indicated in German miles. These miles were also used by the lookout, crying the distance to the coastal area he saw from his high position in the topmast. A German mile (7.408 km, 1/15th latitude) is equivalent to four English nautical miles of 1,852 m (1/60th latitude). The ship's speed was estimated in German miles per hour.

A nautical chart and corresponding sailing instructions were used to determine the course (the sailing direction) at sea. The third mate assigned the chosen course to the helmsman: a seaman whose duty it was to keep the ship on course with the rudder. The helmsman kept an eye on the compass, and had to steer so that the ship sailed as far as possible in the same direction as the indicated course. The third mate usually had a great deal of experience with sailing on the high seas, and would keep an occasional watch on the course. He not only checked whether the right course was being maintained, but also paid atten-

---

12 The day-to-day life of passengers on East Indiamen is described in a lively manner in the journals of the Lammens and Swellengrebel sisters (Barend-Van Haeften, 1996). Life on ships without passengers (who brought their own staff to prepare meals) must have been much simpler.

tion to the position of the sails with respect to the wind direction. Having the sails in the correct position reduced the pressure on the rudder, which greatly facilitated the helmsman's work.

To determine the ship's position at sea, nautical charts and various nautical instruments were used, depending on the kind of observations that could be made on board. If the coast was in sight, one or more compass bearings usually sufficed. On the high seas, an octant was used to determine the ship's position. In both cases, the celestial information was noted down and placed on the chart as a dead reckoning plot (a measured position). The nautical chart used on board the *Amstelveen* is described and explained in detail in the next chapter.

16 – Compass of a Dutch East Indiaman by Johannes van Keulen, Amsterdam. A compass rose is divided into four segments of 90° each which are bounded by the four cardinal points of the compass (north, east, south and west) and subdivided into 32 points: eight points in each of the four segments. Clockwise, starting at N(orth): N by E(ast), NNE, NE by N, NE, NE by E, ENE, E by N, and further: E, E by S(outh) and so forth. N by E (north by east) is one point east of north, at a quarter of the 45° arc between N and NE, thus 11.2° east of N. A ship sailing to the NE has NW 'at a right angle' at port (P) and SE 'at a right angle' at starboard (SB). At a right angle means: at 90° to the ship's course. In this case, at P somewhat 'more aft than at a right angle' means: somewhat more to the west than NW. Two points more aft than at a right angle is therefore WNW. On board the *Amstelveen* on 5 August 1763, sailing to the NE, they saw coastland at WSW (i.e. to the west-south-west), so five or six points more aft than at a right angle.

On the *Amstelveen*, both types of bearings were taken on the day of the accident. The compass bearing was inaccurate, however. A strip of coastal land was indeed observed, but no clearly recognisable land feature from which a bearing could be taken; nor was a sounding taken. At that time, the depth of the water was measured with a deep-sea lead: a lead rod on a long line, marked per fathom by knots, which was slung forward underhand by an experienced seaman standing windward. Pulled tightly in a vertical position, the slung line's length gave an indication of the depth of the water.[13] Sounding on a heavily rolling sailing ship was not without its dangers.

To determine the position of a vessel, the crew would use an imaginary worldwide network of coordinates crossing each other at right angles: meridians (great circles across both poles, at right angles to the equator) and parallels (parallel to the equator, across the northern and southern hemispheres). The prime meridian across Greenwich is the best-known meridian today, but on board Dutch ships in the 18th century, the prime meridian on the nautical charts that were used went across Tenerife, 16° 30' farther to the west. The eastern longitude measured on board the *Amstelveen* (72° 55') should thus be reduced by 16° 30' if a contemporary nautical chart is used to analyse the accident.

The route to the Persian Gulf lies in the northern hemisphere. The *Amstelveen* neared the coast of the Arabian Peninsula at lat. 18° N, whereas the customary route of the time took ships to about lat. 22° N. On a north-easterly course, that translates into a sizeable difference of 500 km. Ships that sighted the coast at about lat. 22° N headed for the Gulf of Oman, but remained far from the coast for safety's sake. Why things happened so differently on the *Amstelveen* remains a mystery for now.

On 5 May 1762, the *Amstelveen* embarked on her fifth journey from Texel to Batavia, this time under the command of Captain Nicolaas Pietersen. She stayed in the roadstead of the Cape of Good Hope for a welcome stopover from 4 to 21 September, where fresh water, fruit and vegetables were brought on board. The *Amstelveen* arrived in the roadstead of Batavia on 28 November 1762. While she had made a relatively quick crossing, it had been marred by disaster.[14] Under way, many of those on board had fallen seriously ill. After arrival, another 40 crewmen died in the hospital in Batavia. One of them was

13 The sounding lead had an opening at the bottom, in which tallow could be placed to obtain a sample of the type of sea bottom. However, the 18th-century chart of the south coast of Oman did not contain any information about the type of sea bottom. Given this, it did not make much sense to use a deep-sea lead containing tallow.
14 The outward voyage took 190 nautical days in total, whereas the ships that sailed from Texel to Batavia between 1760 and 1780 took 210 nautical days on average (H. Bonke, 1999, p. 44).

Jan van Oorschot was a prominent official: an extraordinary member of the Council of Justice in Batavia. He was most likely travelling to Kharg on business, probably a secret mission.

According to the ledger of the Amstelveen, he sailed as a high-ranking, well-paid VOC servant on the fifth outward voyage of the Amstelveen for the first time to the East Indies. This means that he already knew Captain Pietersen well. However, in the archive nothing more could be found on this judge and the purpose of his voyage to Kharg. His mission may have been connected with the desertion of the former resident of Kharg, Jan van der Hulst, Buschman's predecessor. Jan van der Hulst defected to the English with a substantial sum of money and left Persia by ship under English protection. He had already been sentenced by Batavia and banished for life from the charter area of the VOC. Batavia urged Buschman to recover as much of the stolen money as possible and to convert Van der Hulst's possessions to cash to compensate for the loss suffered.

Eyks did not mention the presence of Jan van Oorschot on board of the Amstelveen in his letter to Buschman, and neither does he seem to have informed the Resident about his death. After all, Buschman would certainly have reported the death of such a prominent official to Batavia without delay. His death as a consequence of the wreckage has been recorded in the ledger of the Amstelveen in the VOC archive.

the first mate, Hendrik Wijnboom, who died in Batavia on 2 March 1763.

To transport two large batches of sugar to Kharg in the Persian Gulf, a freighter with a large cargo capacity was needed. The *Amstelveen*, which was anchored in the roadstead of Batavia, was chosen. A largely new crew of 85 souls came on board. Nicolaas Pietersen was again charged with command of the ship. For the first time in his long career, he was not to sail directly back to Holland. Eyks was transferred to the *Amstelveen* and also twenty soldiers boarded to relieve the garrison at Fort Mosselstein. There was only one passenger on board: Jan van Oorschot, an extraordinary member of the Council of Justice in Batavia, most likely travelling to Kharg. Eyks did not mention him in his *Notes*. His presence was, however, documented in the VOC archive in The Hague.

The personal details of almost all drowned seamen and soldiers can be found in the VOC archive. Only the identity of the first mate remains unknown. This might change, if the muster roll for this journey were to be recovered. It is also strange that the first mate was not mentioned by name in the Resolution of the High Government in Batavia, in which the captain and first mate were accused

17 – Ship's manifest of the *Amstelveen* on the way to Kharg (Kareek). Copy in a VOC cargo book: *'Generaal journaal' kept in Batavia 1762–1763*, NA, VOC Archive, inv.no. 10785, p. 97.

of negligence. Is it possible that there was actually no qualified first mate on board? Eyks did report the death of a first mate in his letter to Buschman. Did someone else perhaps fulfil the role? Eyks also reported the death of two old navigators ranked as third mates, but besides Eyks, there were *three* men on board ranked as third mate, according to the Company's personnel records. Eyks' logbook does not offer a decisive answer, but it does give us a number of clues that offer starting points for further research.

Information on the cargo of the *Amstelveen* is specified down to the last detail in the 1762–1763 general register of the VOC's Bookkeeper in Batavia.[15] In the 1990s, this information proved to be of particular interest to divers, following the spectacular auction of the cargo of gold and porcelain that was recovered from the *Amstelveen*'s sister ship, the *Geldermalsen*.[16]

The cargo of the *Amstelveen*, however, consisted mainly of sugar that dis-

15 Dutch East India Company (VOC) Archives, inv. no. 10785.
16 C.J.A. Jörg, *The Geldermalsen. History and Porcelain*. Groningen, 1986.

solved in the sea water, spices that floated away in boxes, sappan wood[17] that washed up on the coast, turmeric that coloured the sea around the wreck yellow for a while, cotton threads from Java which must have got tangled in the breakers and, at the very bottom of the hold, as ballast, a few hundred ingots of tin, which could easily be dug up by beachcombers as soon as the monsoon season was definitely over, five to seven weeks after the ship ran aground. Besides this merchandise, there were some consumer goods for Fort Mosselstein on board: three wooden rulers, two lead containers of ink, a half-vat of bacon, a half vat of resin, 1,500 kilos of rice, a box of medicines, various artillery and armoury articles, iron nails and rifles for the twenty soldiers making the crossing. Everything had been registered.

'If the ship had been wrecked on the return voyage from Kharg, it [finding the wreck] would have been a golden find: large quantities of gold and silver coins were on Kharg waiting to be transported to Batavia'.[18] When Slot wrote these words, it was believed that a diver had recently located the wreck. The wreck was not found, however; the ship had not run aground in that location after all.[19]

Most likely, nothing more can be found of the wreck itself. Reflecting on this, Slot went on to conclude: 'What remains as possible finds are some navigational instruments and metal and earthenware possessions of crewmembers. There are probably still some tin ingots. They might be considered interesting. In 1763, no less, there was a scandal about tampering with tin: ingots of tin were found which were not solid, but consisted of a thin layer of tin over a piece of cheap lead.'[20] Such an ingot would naturally be of real value to a museum, due to the very special story lying behind it.[21]

17 Sappan wood (wood from the sappan tree, *Caesalpinta sappan*) was often used on board as dunnage and then sold as raw material for a red dye.
18 Slot, 1993, p. 8.
19 The location was kept secret to keep others away, but it could nevertheless be found out: it was Sawqirah Beach, at about latitude 18° 10' N, 10 to 15 km north of Hittam.
20 Slot, 1993, p. 8.
21 The letter of 24 May 1764 from the High Government to Kharg made mention of tin '*dat van binnen bevonden is lood te wezen*' (that was found to be lead on the inside). It could still serve as ballast, but was sold nonetheless at any price.

In the Bay of Sawqirah

Long before European ships sailed to Asia, Arabian, Persian and Chinese seamen undertook long-lasting voyages along the extensive coasts of Africa, Arabia, India, Malaysia, Indonesia and China. They preferred to sail in their rather small vessels within good sight of the coast, often using monsoon winds. Their skills were rooted in tradition, courage and experience: they sailed without reliable navigation maps.

European sailors followed the same nautical strategy in the Mediterranean and in the coastal waters of Western Europe. However, in the 14th and 15th centuries, they started to use pilot books and charts made by local mapmakers. These maps were based upon experience, nautical observations recorded in logs of earlier journeys and small geographical sketches mainly made by naval officers. Early charts with sailing directives are known as portolani. A portolano is a nautical chart showing a coastline, on which striking landmarks that could be easily seen from the sea — such as cliffs and ports — were indicated at right angles to the coastline. A portolano offers concrete support for coastal navigation and short open-sea crossings. The sequence of ports was essential, particularly for square-rigged ships. Ideally, these ships would sail with a rear wind (with the wind aft); they could not easily sail against the wind to correct a mistake or navigation error.

In the late 15th century, Spanish and Portuguese navigators developed expertise in oceanic navigation, but still preferred sailing within sight of the coast. Combining both strategies, they sailed round the Cape of Good Hope to India and the Malayan Archipelago, China and Japan; and Columbus discovered America in his attempt to sail to 'India' the other way around. In both countries, cartographers designed new world maps in portolano format, which reflected the results of both coastal and oceanic navigation.

They were soon followed and surpassed by the Dutch. In the 17th century, the cartographers of the VOC and the Dutch WIC — the West-Indian Company, active in the Americas — dominated map making worldwide, often using older maps made by Portuguese cartographers to fill in the gaps in their knowledge of coastal areas that they had never explored and charted themselves. A nice example of this practice of borrowing in the chart-making industry is the mapping of the south coast of the Arabian Peninsula.

In the first half of the 18th century, European maps of the Arabian Peninsula were still made in this way. They were updated occasionally when new informa-

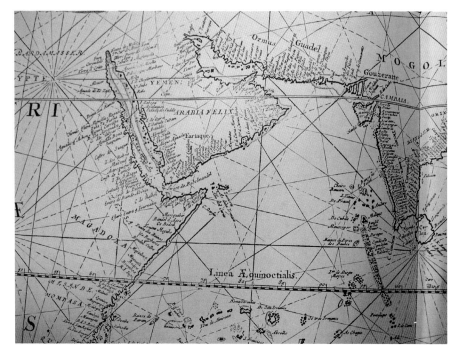

18 – The Arabian Sea, part of an old nautical chart with the coasts still in portolano style. From the *Nieuwe Pascaert van Oostindiën*, a sea chart of the Indian Ocean from the Cape of Good Hope to Tasmania, c. 1680.

tion became available, but due to earlier mistakes and unfounded assumptions, all kinds of errors and confusing fabrications had crept in and were maintained for many decades. The work of nautical cartographers was often far from accurate. Their sources could only give a broad impression of the coasts, and many observations in the logbooks were not based on reliable bearings, soundings and accurate celestial observations.

The nautical officers on the *Amstelveen*, however, had a relative modern nautical chart at their disposal.[22] In the 18th century, such maps enabled a captain to sail safely across the oceans, or along a coast far from shore, using the nautical instruments of the time: an accurate compass and an octant for celestial positioning. This obviated the need to sail close to a dangerous coast, so as to keep land in sight. The Arabian coast was known to be a perilous coast. Despite this, Captain Pietersen seems to have been intent on doing so.

The old navigation method — sailing with the coast in sight, aided by a portolano chart — may have played a part in the accident involving the *Amstelveen*. After passing Ceylon and the Maldives to the south of the equator, the ship crossed the Arabian Sea in a north-north-westerly direction. It neared, how-

22 Probably the printed nautical chart by Johannes van Keulen (Gawronski, 1996, p. 229). They sometimes used an updated copy of such a chart that had been made in Batavia.

Van Batavia naar de Mallabaar, en van daar na Suratte, Persië en Mocha.

De Schepen die in de Maand November na deze Plaatsen willen vertrekken / houden de coers met de Cylonsche Schepen tot dat Eyland / van waar zy naar de Mallabaar overstellen / en verders langs de wal na Suratte en Persië strevenen / of de coers Westwaarts naar Mocha stellen : maar indien zy in de Maand van September of October t'zeyl gaan / moeten zy in de Z. O. passaat zo Westelyk lopen / tot dat Punte Gale Noorden van hen is / en van afhoudende de coers zo Westelyk aanstellen / dat zy benoosten de Maldives, en bewesten Cylon blyvende de hoogte houden / om niet met de Westelyke winden / die thans in November nog benoorden de Linie worden gevonden / en met de Oostwaarts vallende stromen benoosten Cylon te worden gezet / daar zy zo lang zouden moeten sukkelen / tot de Z. O. Moussen hen eindelyk daar van verloste. En alschoon het gebeurde / dat de Z. O. Moussen broeger door kennende / en zy nog bewesten Cylon zig bebonden / zo kan de Mallabaar evenwel by hen worden bestevent / en van daar de coers naar de gemelde Comptoiren worden gestelt / op zulk een wyze als hier voor in de beschryving van dat Vaarwater gezegt is.

Maar de Schepen die naar Persië of Suratte gedestineert / in de Maanden van Juny en July van Batavia vertrekken / houden bewesten de Maldives en in 't Vaarwater der Cylonsche Schepen van dien tyd / tot onder de Linie, van waar de eerstgemelde de coers N. N. W. op de Arabische kust aan hebben te stellen / en langs dezelve naar de Persische Zeeboezem afhouden / en de laastgemelde de coers Noorden behoudende / tot op de breette van de Suratsche Zeeboezem / van Oost aanstevenen naar de gemelde Plaats.

19 – Sailing directions for the route to the Persian Gulf in the nautical atlas *Zee Fakkel*, Johannes van Keulen, 1753. The last paragraph applies to the course of the Amstelveen: 'But the ships that leave Batavia for Persia and Suratte in the months of June and July first follow the same course as ships that are bound for Ceylon at this time. They continue until they are west of the Maldives. Directly below the equator, ships bound for Persia follow a NNW course until they come to the Arabian Coast, and then sail further along this coast to the Persian Gulf. Ships that are bound for Suratte sail north from the equator until they reach the latitude of the coastal waters near Suratte, and then sail eastwards to their destination.'

ever, the coast of Oman at about lat. 18° N; perhaps somewhat more to the north, but at any rate much more to the south than indicated in the sailing instructions for a voyage to the Persian Gulf. According to these, a captain had to approach the south coast of the Arabian Peninsula at approximately lat. 22° N, thus far to the north of the island of Masirah. From there, the Gulf of Oman could be reached by sailing northwards at a safe distance from that coast to Ras al Hadd, the easternmost Cape of Oman at lat. 23° N. See map on p. 91.

Two independent sources state that the ship had reached the south coast 'after a successful voyage.'[23] The difference of four degrees latitude cannot reasonably be ascribed to adverse winds, poor steering or navigational errors. Captain Pietersen must have intentionally deviated from the normal route. The captain may have sought out the wind in order to benefit as soon as possible from the south-westerly monsoon along the south coast. This monsoon wind subsides at the end of August, and is followed by a period of weak, changeable winds. Eyks knew this, and he was even able to tell Naraitun the date on which the monsoon would turn.

Was Captain Pietersen in a hurry? Certainly, he would have wanted to reach the Persian Gulf as quickly as possible, and even said so explicitly to Eyks on Friday, 5 August, at the change of the evening watch. Those must have been some of his last words on the poop deck before the ship ran aground three hours later. It remains unclear whether, on departure from Batavia, Pietersen had been given permission (or had indeed been instructed) to deviate from the prescribed route for the sake of a faster crossing. This may well have been the case, given Batavia's frustration with 'the snail's pace'[24] at which ships sailed on the route to the Persian Gulf and back. Or did Captain Pietersen perhaps himself decide to take an alternative, hopefully faster, route? There are also reasons why this may have been the case. No doubt, the one and only passenger on board was also in a hurry. There was a lot at stake.

On Thursday, 4 August, towards the evening, the ship ended up in the monsoon and the course was changed to the north-east. That night, they had the wind aft as they sailed along the south coast, probably much closer to land than they thought. The *Amstelveen* had a depth of four fathoms (seven metres). The chart on board warned against shallow areas in the bay to the north of Cape Mataraca, but not against similar dangers in the large Bay of Sawqirah, in which they were sailing. On the contrary, the map gave the impression that this bay was easily navigable, and that a ship could sail in sight of the coast in clear weather. This was exactly what Captain Pietersen had in mind, and it was this strategy that he plainly advocated to Eyks.

The next morning, after the mist had lifted and the sun was shining again, they saw a strip of coastal land on the quarter behind them to the west-south-west, at a distance of 5.5–6 German miles (about 45 km). From the topmast (high up in the foremast), nothing was to be seen to the north. As they did not sight any land in front (the direction in which they were sailing), they presumed that the coastland they saw in the distance was the coast of Cape Mata-

23 Eyks' logbook and the record of the interrogation of the seamen Brinkhout and Poolman.
24 On 24 May 1764, even penal measures against 'voyages at a snail's pace' were enacted.

20 – Arabian cormorants (*Phalacrocorax nigrogularis*) are usually called Socotra cormorants. They forage along the coast between Masirah and Dhofar in the south (M. Gallagher & M.W. Woodcock, 1980, p. 60) and breed on the ground in the desert, as was recently discovered by the makers of the BBC television series, Planet Earth.

raca. In view of their expectation that they would soon be able to see the Cape, the coastline on the chart they were using on board and the Captain's expressed wish to reach the Gulf as quickly as possible, this was a plausible notion. None of the ship's mates questioned this. However, this daring assumption was at odds with the day's celestial observations. At the changing of the watch at noon, it had been determined that they were at lat. 18° 40' N, while their eastern longitude had indicated that they were sailing rather close to the Arabian coast. In that position, it would not have been possible to see Cape Mataraca 'far away,' abaft the beam, on the quarter behind them. The captain apparently had more faith in what he could see (and in his unconfirmed assumption that it was Cape Mataraca, which is what he wanted to see) than in the celestial observations made with the octant on the heavily rolling ship.

That afternoon, they sailed on from lat. 18° 40' N in a north-easterly direction. On the poop, the signals indicating that they might be sailing in shallow water were ignored. They saw large numbers of cormorants. Seamen who had been close to the Arabian coast more often (but further north) had never seen this before. Cormorants, it should be noted, only dive in shallow coastal water. However, in order to measure the depth of the water with the deep-sea lead, the ship's speed would have to be reduced. Owing to the high waves and the weak condition of the old ship, the captain considered it better not to do so. The ship sailed ahead too fast, and rolled heavily in the strangely high breakers. Sounding would have been too dangerous. At a lower speed, the waves coming from behind would have posed a serious threat to the weak stern. At the changing of the evening watch, the captain explicitly repeated this to Eyks, whose duty as third mate was to assist the first mate during the evening watch between 8 p.m. and midnight. Months later, in his *Notes*, Eyks would write down what the captain had told him at the changing of the watch, and what had happened afterwards. Strangely enough, in the following pages he did not say a word about the captain (who had probably gone to sleep) and the first mate (the watch officer).

In the course of the evening, the fog rose again and the wind died down. It became impossible to keep the ship on course in the high breakers (which were in fact ground swells). The ship suddenly hit the hard, sandy bottom. After some time, she became stuck and capsized onto her starboard side. That night, everyone on board realised that the ship was lost. The masts were cut down and all manner of things were thrown overboard in the hope that the ship would right herself again and come to lie somewhat higher on the sandy bank.

The next morning, the sailors' initial thought was that they had run aground somewhere in the Bay of Enzaädades Baixos, the Old Portuguese name for the shallow Gulf of Masirah, north of Cape Mataraca. After the fog had lifted, however, they saw a low beach in front of them. This was not compatible with their position of the evening before.[25] Meanwhile, the high breakers continued to pound the low middle deck. The longboat, which they had made ready for a rescue the night before, was still there, but it would only end up in the water

25 They estimated the evening before at sundown (6.30 p.m.) that they were 49 minutes (49 nautical miles, 90 km) from the island of Masirah and already 8 miles (German miles of 7.4 km, so almost 60 km) from the coast.

if the ship were to be hit by a huge breaking wave. In the chaos, all on board feared for the worst and prayed for deliverance.

Early in the morning of Sunday, 7 August 1763, only a day-and-a-half after the ship had run aground, the poop of the *Amstelveen* broke into pieces. The quarterdeck behind the large mast also disappeared into the waves. In the process, four of the eight men standing on it were drowned. Then the boatswain (Jonas Daalberg) and a seaman brought themselves to safety with a boom (a spar by which a yard is extended). From the forecastle of the ship, the other sailors saw them arrive safely on the beach. Shortly afterwards, a high wave knocked the longboat overboard and filled it with water. The next wave capsized the longboat, and all but two sitting in it were drowned. The captain's chest was also lost at that moment. Then the portside up to the foredeck was washed away. The entire fragment along with four heavy cannons drifted onto the beach. By then, the *Amstelveen* had largely disappeared into the waves.

Eyks and many of the crew, mostly seamen, were still sitting on a piece of the forecastle. They placed all their hopes on the bowsprit and the spritsail yard, sitting atop of them and trying to loosen or cut the wooldings and bobstays, along with everything else that was still fastened by ropes and might get in their way. At about 9 o'clock, the bowsprit, 'full of people,' fell into the water, but remained somehow attached to the ship. A huge wave pulled Eyks under twice. When he surfaced, he was able to grab some rope that was hanging down from the fore of the ship. His aim was to climb up against the ship's bows, aided by the boatswain's mate and a seaman, but he was prevented from doing so by the weight of his clothes. He asked the two men to cut the soaking tailcoat from his body. They did so, but when he looked round, the bowsprit, and everyone who had been sitting or holding on to it, had drifted away. Immediately afterwards, heavy breakers [ground swell] arose, smashing the remainder of the fore part of the ship to pieces.

The men were now floating in the water amongst the pieces of wreckage, attempting to reach the coast right through the breakers 'with God's help and guidance.' They made their way in the waves from one piece to another. Eyks clutched as many as six pieces of driftwood before he reached the shore. He had great difficulty in getting onto the beach. He was rolled back into the sea three times, his body constantly smashing against the wood of the wreck that had washed onto the beach and that was dashing his body to pieces, as it were. He almost collapsed from the pain and called for help. His cries were answered by three men, who pulled him across the masts, topmasts and pieces of wreckage, and laid him down in the sand.

As Eyks recalled in his logbook, he lay completely unconscious, with a cut in his head and a wound above his left eye. His arms and legs looked as if they had been flayed, and other parts of his body were in still worse shape. He did not lie there for long, however; a short while later, he saw the surgeon and the boatswain coming towards him. They asked if any other officers, such as the captain or navigators, had arrived on the shore. 'Whereupon they received the answer: I am here!' He added immediately: 'But they did not think I would survive.' Had he already recovered from the initial shock of the accident?

The boatswain and the bay man (the surgeon's second mate) then came to take a closer look at Eyks. The bay man bound Eyks' wounds, and the boatswain laid him on his back against a small sand dune. Some seamen removed his wet clothes and put dry clothes on him, and the boatswain and a few other seamen fetched boards to set up a tent as protection against the wind and dew. Around noon, exhausted, and feeling as if he had been drawn and quartered under water, Eyks fell into a deep sleep.

That evening, the boatswain mustered the crew. Jonas Daalberg was accustomed to keeping an overview in dire circumstances and asserting his authority. He concluded officially and solemnly on the beach that 'through the Lord's providence and mercy, we with 30 souls have remained in the land of the living.' In his *Notes*, Eyks listed the survivors as follows:

21 – Breakers on Cape Mataraca. Area c. 600 × 900 m, eye level 850 m. This image was captured on 16 June 2004. In the middle of June, the distance between the crests of the waves at the coast is already more than 80-100 metres. In July and the first half of August, this distance is even greater, and the waves are thus even higher.

'I, Cornelis Eyks, Third Mate

1   Jonas Daalberg, Boatswain
1   Pieter Coene, Surgeon's Second Mate
1   Pieter van Holland, Boatswain's Second Mate
1   Hans Lutjes, Assistant Cook
21   Seamen
3   Soldiers
1   Little Black Boy
—

Thus 30 Souls.'

Then, in a short review of events, Eyks summarised what happened on that fateful day and what could be seen on the beach. The captain, other officers and the remaining crew had 'all died, and none of the dead were recognisable because most of them had lost their arms, legs, heads etc.: it was heart-breaking to behold those who had fallen victim to this disastrous fate.'

Several of those who had escaped death were injured. That night, a watch was kept. Finally, Eyks sighed that he thought the Lord wanted to put an end to his life that night, because he had such heavy stitches in his side that he could hardly breathe. Even a navigator can sometimes end up in troubled waters.

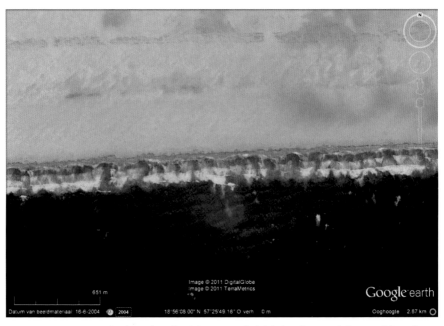

22 – Cape Mataraca. The huge beach with extremely high breakers and the small low dunes where Eyks fell into a deep sleep. Area c. 1,9 × 2,8 km, eye level 2,9 km.

The next morning, however, it emerged that nine pigs and a cow had also made it to the shore alive without the aid of driftwood. That makes one stop and think. The waves had undoubtedly been fearsomely high and rough, but the *Amstelveen* had clearly not broken apart far from the coast. If it had, the animals would certainly not have survived. Why, then, had so many men died?

There was yet another question. On board everyone had thought it a secondary issue, but once safe and sound on the beach, no one could avoid it. They were still alive and on an ostensibly safe, quiet and desolate beach near a dreary, empty, barren, horrifying desert, somewhere on the immense south coast of Arabia.

But where? How could they find out? And what next? Where should they go?

We will now take a small leap forward in time, before returning to Eyks' account of his amazing survival journey along the desert coast of Oman.

Two old letters

Three months after running aground, Cornelis Eyks, the only officer to survive the disaster, reported the accident to Resident Buschman[26] on Kharg, a small island in the Persian Gulf with a walled trading post, Fort Mosselstein. Eyks had written to Buschman almost immediately after arriving in Muscat to inform him about what had happened, but the letter had not yet arrived on Kharg; that is why he gave Buschman his copy. The VOC's archives contain two copies (inv.nos. 3123/8298) of this unique letter, in which Eyks gives a concise and clear impression of the mysterious accident's impact.

To My Lord
Mr Bosman, Merchant and Manager in Kharg

Your Lordship is hereby informed that the Ship Amstelveen, *Captain Nicolaas Pieterzen, commissioned to sail from Batavia to Kharg, ran aground on 5 August 1763 at N. Latitude 18 deg. 40 m. at ten thirty at night in heavy breakers; broke apart on the 7th of this month at 9 o'clock, whereby 75 of the 105 souls on board drowned, including the Captain, First Mate and Chief Petty Officer and two old navigators and for the rest officers, sailors and soldiers. So 30 of us escaped, and after 31 days' travel, 8 of us arrived at Muscat on 11 September at the Agent's.*[27]
Concerning the cargo of our ship, very little of it could be seen on the beach, nor could it be approached owing to the heavy breakers. We think we will stay here another three days to fill our hungry stomachs and allow our burnt bodies to rest.

Yours respectfully, Your Faithful Servant,
Cornelis Eyks, Third Mate of the Ship Amstelveen

Muscat, 11 September 1763.

---

26 Willem Bosman changed his name to Buschman after being promoted to Resident.
27 The Company's agent in Muscat, Naraitun, a trader and charterer. Naraitun accommodated various survivors of the *Amstelveen* in his house with ancillary warehouse in Muscat.

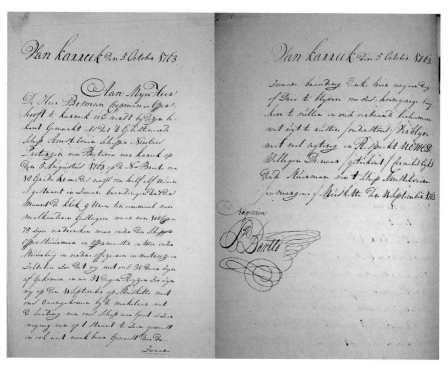

23 – Copy of the letter of Cornelis Eyks to Mr Bosman, Merchant and Chief at Kareek (Kharg), dated September 11th, 1763. NA, VOC Archive, inv.no. 8298, p. 20-21.

According to Eyks, there had been 105 'souls' on board, of whom 75 were said to have drowned: the captain, first mate, surgeon, two old navigators and the other officers, as well as seamen and soldiers. There were only 30 survivors: 29 Europeans and a little Javanese slave boy. The latter perhaps served as a cabin boy for Captain Pietersen and his high-ranking passenger, Jan van Oorschot, a member of the VOC's Council of Justice in Batavia. Van Oorschot also died, but Eyks made no mention of this in his letter to Buschman. It is also striking that Eyks did not make any reference to the tremendously difficult, terrifying journey along the barren desert coast. He was also silent about the exact location of the wreck.

Buschman received Eyks immediately after he arrived on Kharg. Eyks told him what had happened and approximately where the ship had been lost. This is evident from a letter that Resident Buschman wrote to Batavia the next day. Copies of this elegant letter have also been saved (inv.nos. 3123/8298).

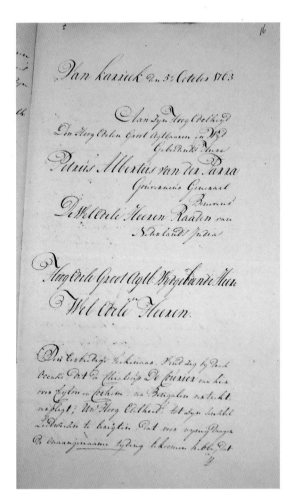

24 – First page of the missive from Resident Buschman to Batavia, October 5th, 1763, announcing the loss of the Amstelveen on the coast of Cape Mataraca (Ras Madrakah). Copy, NA, VOC Archief, inv.no. 8298, p. 16-19.

To the Highly Esteemed
Noble Excellency and Wide Commanding Lord Petrus Albertus van der
Parra, Governor General
As well as Their Excellencies the Lords of the Council of Dutch East Indies.

Highly Esteemed Excellency and Wide Commanding Lord,
Your Excellencies,

The respectful signatory, on the occasion of the departure of the sloop DE
COURIER *from here to Bengal by way of Ceylon and Cochim,*[28] *is compelled,*
to his great sorrow, to notify your Esteemed Excellency that a few days ago,
he received the bad tidings that the commissioned Ship the AMSTELVEEN,
Capt. Nicolaas Pietersen, departing from Batavia to this location, on 5 Aug.

28 Cochin on the south-west coast of India. Buschman wrote Cochim, as Eyks did in his
Notes.

last, *sailing at a latitude of 18 degrees 40 minutes between Cape Mataraca*
and Curia Muria, ran aground at night, to such an extent that nothing could
be salvaged of the entire cargo and even all wage papers were lost. Of the 105
Europeans on board, 75 unfortunately drowned and 30 floated to land on piec-
es of driftwood, of whom only 8 made it to Muscat, and subsequently arrived
here: a Third Mate, a Boatswain's Second Mate and 6 ordinary seamen.
The two first-mentioned, who cannot be employed here, will go along with the
bringer of this message.

The remaining crew, whom they had to leave behind in a lamentable condi-
tion, and who had separated themselves from the others in order to find their
own shelter, were brazenly murdered[29] or died through lack of provisions,
according to the Navigator.

The Agent Naraitoen, having heard first from the Navigator that some pieces
of artillery could still be seen on the beach, rented a vessel which departed
thither with a galley of Sheikh's Caliphate to pick up said artillery etc.

The short time of 2 days that this vessel was here does not allow me to send
the books to Your Excellency which are now being prepared. I have therefore
enclosed for Your Excellency's consideration a Yield Statement of the sale,
referring for the rest to the missive sent with RENSWOUDE *subject to favour-*
able tides, of which a duplicate is enclosed, and further having the honour to
inform Your Excellency that everything at this trading post is in good condi-
tion and at peace, but that not much improvement can be found in the trade
since my last missive, although in 4 months' time, more has been sold than I
had imagined, which it will please Your Excellencies to see from the above-
mentioned Yield Statement.

The troubles and confusion in these neighbouring provinces still continue, but
the roads to Basra, Baghdad and across those places to Persia are open again.
I shall therefore look forward to seeing another Ship in the month of March
or April, as little remains of desired merchandise owing to this fatal incident,
so the sale thereof can hardly make up the charges and expenses of the current
financial year, as no Ship has arrived by way of Malabar.

For the rest, as time does not allow me to give Your Excellencies a more
detailed account, I shall have the honour, with the most profound esteem and
performance of my duties ...
[after considerable ceremony etc.]
    W.J. Buschman, Kharg in Fort Mosselstein, the 5th of October 1763.

---

29 *Assurant* is an old Zeeland (South Netherlands) word. It means 'too self-assured,
cheeky'; *van assurantie* means 'brazenly'. Eyks presented both causes of death as possibili-
ties, not as something about which one could say anything with certainty.

Buschman's letter contains more detail, but essentially offers the same account of the event. The last part of the letter reveals the Resident's view of the political situation that influenced his trade in the Gulf region. It is striking that, unlike Eyk's letter, Buschman's letter mentions the location of the shipwreck. The coast between Cape Mataraca and the Curia Muria Islands is however at least 300 km long. Eyks did not know exactly where the wreck was located, but he did know where he could find it. Moreover, he knew that he was not the only one to know this; there were even ships already under way to the location of the accident...

What Eyks told the Resident about the location differs considerably from what he (like the captain and the other navigators) had assumed before and shortly after the ship ran aground. He still remembered it exactly, and subsequently recorded it carefully in his *Notes*. At that time, he had clearly known that something had not been quite right, but did he already know why they had run aground so suddenly?

Just like Eyks, Buschman did not make further reference to the cause of the disaster. Did Eyks keep silent on this point out of reverence or prudence, or was something else going on? Did Eyks himself have a clear idea about this?

Moreover, what had actually happened during the voyage to Muscat? Had castaways been killed, as Buschman seems to suggest? Had Eyks been naïve and let information slip, both here and in Hadd and Muscat? These are difficult questions, and they bring us back to the wreck and to the start of the miraculous survival journey made by a large group of destitute seamen along the southern desert coast of Oman, and the curious logbook that Eyks during the next months wrote about the shipwreck and their unprecedented journey in the late summer of 1763.

At Cape Mataraca (Ras Madrakah)

The disaster occurred at Cape Mataraca, a spit of land in the Arabian Sea that was called *Cabo Matracha* on the nautical maps used by Portuguese seamen. Corruptions of this old Portuguese name[30] appeared on nautical charts drawn by cartographers from other European seafaring nations until well into the 18th century: Spain, Holland, England and France. On the Dutch map on board the *Amstelveen*, the cape looked like a hooked peninsula.

For centuries, Cape Mataraca was of practical importance to the Arabs who sailed along the south coast of Oman. The cape extends far into the sea and can easily be seen from afar most of the time. On the north side, there is a sheltered anchorage for ships on their way to Muscat and the Arabian Gulf, returning from Salalah in Dhofar, Mocha in Yemen, Jeddah in the Red Sea or Zanzibar off the east coast of Africa. For these ships and for other small vessels coming from the south in the monsoon season, Cape Mataraca was a favourite shelter for the night. The sea swell is interrupted by barren cliffs; waves break against them into bright white bubbling foam. On the north side, the sea becomes almost level and the swell light and pleasant.

To the west, Mataraca soon becomes broader and the cliffs a little higher. There is a narrow beach on the south side, wedged between rugged masses of rocks. Farther to the west, except for a lagoon where many birds gather, there is nothing but sand running along the sea: an immeasurable beach curving to the south in a wide arc. The sun glitters on the clear water of the Bay of Sawqirah. On the north side, there is the Gulf of Masirah, named after the island of Masirah[31] to the north-east. The Portuguese called this bay Enzaädades Baixos (shallow inlet). Here, little of the monsoon is noticeable after mid-August. It is very hot in the late summer, with the daytime temperature sometimes rising as high as 54° Celsius.

The day after the accident, when it was still foggy, it was suspected on board that the *Amstelveen* had run aground somewhere in this huge bay. But after the mist had risen and the sun began to shine again, they realised that they

---

30 On the chart on board the AMSTELVEEN, *Caab Materaca* was written; on the poop deck, it was called *Caap Mataraca*. Eyks also wrote *Mataraca*. Nowadays, the official name is Ras Madrakah.

31 Eyks wrote *Maziera*; *Mazia* is written on the nautical chart of Johannes van Keulen (1753).

must be somewhere else. What had happened, and where might they be? Eyks' logbook gave no definite answer. It only became clear to me after an analysis of the terrain that they had to cope with during their walk along the rocky desert coast.

Eyks left us a *personal* logbook. He wrote in the language of his time, but it nevertheless gives a lively impression of what he and 'his people' experienced day after day along the rocky desert coast. Guided by Eyks' *Notes*, in what follows, the account of the trek is retold in modern language and — where necessary — supplemented by statements, considerations and brief explanations, in footnotes and boxes as well as in the text itself. Now and then, for the sake of readability, passages from the logbook are quoted verbatim.

MONDAY, 8 AUGUST 1763

Eyks awoke early in the morning on the beach where he had been washed ashore on the previous day. The long night's rest had done him good. He was still exhausted, but fortunately he had dry clothes, and the windscreen protected him from the chilly air. Relieved, he took a look around. He still felt pain throughout his body, but that would undoubtedly fade away. He had escaped with his life — he was saved, as he thankfully and solemnly wrote down in his *Notes*. This sense of relief put him in a gentle mood, and restored his courage and strength.

On board, he had already seen that the seemingly endless beach ran from east to west. He immediately realised that they could not have run aground in the shallow bay past Cape Mataraca. They had, after all, seen the Cape in the distance in the afternoon of the previous day, and had already left it behind. They had sailed in the dark to the northeast, in the direction of Maziera (Masirah), a large island in the north-east of the Enzaädades Baixos Bend at lat. 20° 20' N. Their position at 6.30 p.m. showed that they still had 49 minutes [degree minutes] to go at sundown. They would not reach Maziera until it was light again. The island was too far away, even if they had the benefit of some current.[32]

In an instant, after he sat up, it occurred to him to take another look at where he had ended up and who else was on the shore. The weather was unchanged, cool and misty. A moderate wind blew in from the sea and there were still strong waves on the coast. Fortunately, the boatswain's mate had also been able to reach the shore. In the chaos on board, Eyks had not eaten anything. Now, however, he was quite thirsty, probably due to all the salt water. He did not note down what he had to eat and drink, but he quickly made a consid-

32 After the ship ran aground, soundings were taken and some current in a northerly direction was determined. On the modern nautical chart BA 3785, a north-easterly current of at least one nautical mile (2 km) an hour is indicated for August.

erable recovery. Had he perhaps been too pessimistic about the extent of his injuries?

The same day, Eyks took a walk some way along the shore with the boatswain and six other men, to see if they could find anything. They were disappointed. They found mostly empty or half-empty casks, a few half-full vats of arak (brandy) and wine, kegs of coconut and sweet oil, a barrel of meat, a keg of French beans, a barrel of sauerkraut, two kegs of sausages and a barrel that still contained some flour. They also found boxes of spices that had burst open in the water, and some rope, which they rolled up as far as they could on the beach.

They also saw the nine pigs and the cow that had survived the breakers. They caught one of the pigs and slaughtered it. As they did not yet have fire, they attempted to make it by rubbing two sticks together long enough for the friction to cause them to spark; this eventually worked. They got some water out of a barrel they found on the beach. They also found the broken-off part of the port with four cannons (eight-pounders) and various other large pieces of wreckage from the ship. All night long, they kept a close watch. Eyks had taken a good look around, but said very little. So many men had died; had that really needed to happen? They, however, were safe, and were now completely on their own. Not a soul could be seen, although they did see that people, probably fishermen, had been there some time ago. Their first task would thus be to become more familiar with their surroundings. Did anyone actually live there?

TUESDAY, 9 AUGUST

The wind and weather were the same as the day before. Eyks, the boatswain and five seamen made a journey inland, arriving in a completely unknown and rather monotonous landscape. Eyks did not record how far they went and how long the journey took. What he wrote down shows his disappointment: they did not meet anyone. While they saw that 'several people' had been there, they did not see anyone.

They had noticed the day before on the beach that people sometimes went there. Various and sundry parts of vessels were piled up against the low dunes. These vessels were sewn together in the same way as the sewn boats on the coast of Coromandel. There were also masts and shrouds, fishing nets, pieces of palliases, hats and pots.

As they did not see anything but cliffs and sand inland, they simply went back. On the beach they heard from other men that they had seen five camels and two pariah dogs[33] walking towards the west.

33 'Pariah dogs', explained Eyks between brackets, are a kind of large, thin dogs we know as 'greyhounds'. Wild dogs were also called pariah dogs.

25 – They did not see anything but cliffs and sand...

WEDNESDAY, 10 AUGUST

The weather and wind remained unchanged. At this point, Eyks must have realised that his account was becoming very monotonous. At sea, the weather would have been a primary concern, but here it was irrelevant. His logbook was not a ship's log, and as he now had other concerns, he left the weather for what it was.

In the morning, the boatswain's mate, Pieter van Holland, was sent ahead to walk inland, accompanied by seven seamen. Afterwards, he reported that they had found a footpath leading to the west. They had seen clear tracks and concluded that several people had walked on it.

It is interesting that Eyks made no mention of exploration in an easterly direction. Was that direction blocked by rocks or by a lagoon that was connected to the sea? Or was this because they had seen camels walking in a westerly direction? The real reason soon became apparent. During their inland journey on Tuesday, Eyks and the boatswain Jonas Daalberg must have consulted one another about what to do. Perhaps then they agreed upon an outline of a plan to escape from the beach shortly after that walk. Eyks did not note down what they discussed, but that can be gleaned from indications in other parts of the text.

Shortly after Pieter van Holland's return, they seem to have decided that they would leave the beach the next day and head towards the inhabited world: to Muscat. Eyks did not note down how and by whom this decision was made. The two men got along well, and must have had a thorough understanding of the situation.

Two questions are important in this respect. First, where exactly had they run aground? The answer to this question would, after all, determine the route they would have to take, obviously without recourse to either a chart or a compass. We will never know who was the first to realise that they had washed ashore on Cape Mataraca, but it is evident from the direction they chose on departure that there was agreement on this. Eyks knew the nautical chart of the area from his time on board, and of course he remembered the bent shape of the spit of land. Walking along the sea in an easterly direction would have been an enormous detour, and might not even have been possible, due to the route being blocked by cliffs.

The path to the west, which had already been explored by the boatswain's mate, would in a short time bring them to a path in a north-easterly direction. Taking this would enable them to take a shortcut to the Gulf of Maziera (Masirah). From there, they would have to go farther north and north-east, close to the shore, always as far as possible across the beach, with the sun on the right-hand side.

There is one indication that Eyks had already questioned the captain's decision on board — after they had sighted coastland behind them — to keep to a northerly course (north by east, for at least two hours before noon) so they could see more land. This was not an illogical decision in itself. Captain Pietersen wanted to be sure that coastland would not be sighted again north of the coastland that they had taken for Cape Mataraca. This is, after all, impossible while sailing away from a cape towards the sea. Eyks nevertheless described that course (north by east) very aptly as 'audacious'; these days, we would say 'rather daring,' or 'too self-assured'. In Eyks' view, too little attention was paid to the alarming results of their celestial positioning. Their position indicated that they were hugging the shore at 18° 40', but they did not see the shore. Did the captain perhaps suspect that their observed celestial position was incorrect? This was a common occurrence on a strongly rolling ship. At that time, due to defective chronometry, taking the longitude on board often led to inaccurate outcomes. On the *Amstelveen*, at about noon, long. 75° 55' E was determined.[34] If they had taken this observation seriously, the men would have realised that they were indeed hugging the shore. Any ship that sails to the north-east that close to the coast runs the risk of running aground on the south side of Cape Mataraca, which must have been what happened on that foggy evening. Eyks' exploration of the seemingly-endless beach with the boatswain, Jonas Daalberg, strengthened their conviction that this is what had occurred. Although it still seemed strange: on the day of the accident, the fog had lifted in the morning, the sun had shone fully again and they had seen coastland at

34 Plotted on a modern nautical chart, this even comes down to a position several miles inland (thus in the desert). See part of map BA 3785 on p. 131.

6 miles (45 km) on the quarter behind them. In front, there had been nothing to see all day long.

Second, who would assume the role of leader? The group was composed mainly of seamen. Jonas Daalberg, an experienced boatswain from Hamburg, had supervised the seamen undertaking deck duty on board. On the beach, he also emerged as an obvious leader. He acted as a contact for the men and organised their activities on the beach. Eyks, however, as the only naval officer who had survived the disaster, was entitled to be the overall leader as a matter of course. Fortunately, the two men got along well and respected the hierarchical relationship between them. They worked together harmoniously and in a well-considered manner for almost the whole of the journey.

How their intention to leave the beach early on Thursday morning was presented to the other survivors is not known, but everyone must have responded with relief. The dismal beach with the remains of drowned crewmembers had become intolerable to all of them. Nor was there much water left that was fit to drink, and the supply of food was also shrinking rapidly.

After the boatswain's mate returned, they made haste with the necessary preparations. As they had run out of food, they searched for the pigs and cow, but failed to find the animals. At around noon, however, the pigs came to them on their own. The men succeeded in catching and slaughtering one of the pigs, which was then made ready for the journey. They also filled their vats and casks — Eyks did not record what they put in them — and got everything ready for departure the next morning. According to their own estimates, they had food for two or three days. That day, they saw two pariah dogs, and they again kept a close watch at night.

Forsaken in the desert

THURSDAY, 11 AUGUST

When the sun rose, they went on their way, calling on Jehovah's blessing, aid and assistance. The boatswain mustered the group: there were still 29 Europeans and one black boy, in accordance with the list he had made earlier. They took along food and drinks for two or three days and a clean set of clothes for each man. They marched that day until sunset, seeing nothing but sandy and rocky land dotted with a few thorn trees.[35] Eyks did not record whether, as was customary on board, they had eaten at noon, or whether they still had to do so at twilight. In the midst of this empty, unknown environment, they lay down to rest. They kept a close watch all night long and sounded the drum,[36] which had also washed up on the beach.

FRIDAY, 12 AUGUST

The men trekked further the next day. Once again, they marched all day long, but encountered no one and saw nothing that differed from the previous day: just sand and rocky land. Apparently, they did not see any animals either. Eyks did not record whether they followed a path or simply walked in a certain direction. Eyks would later put his strategy into words, and this shows that they constantly tried to walk to the north-east, in the direction in which the sun rose.

Again, Eyks confined himself to highlighting the most anxious time of the day: sleeping in the open air. On board, they had often done this during calm, warm nights, and this usually suited them excellently. It was a lot cooler on deck than below. However, here in the frightening desert, sleeping in the open air was an entirely different matter. On board they had been sure that it was safe; here, they had to wait and see. Anyhow, they again kept a sharp watch.

SATURDAY, 13 AUGUST

They continued their march at dawn, but things became difficult as the day progressed. Many men began to complain about stiffness and moaned that

---

35 Relatively small low trees (Acacia) that provide some shade; stopping places for Bedouin.
36 The drum was used on board in case of fog (so others would know they were there). One can only guess at the reason they used it here as well.

they could no longer keep up with the others. They walked barefoot, carrying a bundle of clothes on a stick on one shoulder and a keg or jug on the other. The further they went, the more cliffs they encountered, and there was increasingly less sand to walk on. Walking barefoot over gradually higher, hard rocks; it was not as easy as one would think. They were also entirely unused to walking for so long without a break. Moreover, they had not eaten that day, because they only had food with them for one more day.

After sundown, they went to sleep again, keeping a close watch.

SUNDAY, 14 AUGUST

The men started their march at daybreak. Not long afterwards, a seaman lay down where he was, saying he would rather die where he was than go on, because he saw no way out and could not live without food or drink. This is all that Eyks mentioned of the incident. This might indicate indifference, respect for someone else's decision, and perhaps his embarrassment at the situation. We will never know. It is highly unlikely that they did not at least stop awhile and pray for him.

For the boatswain, too, leaving a man behind must have felt like something of a defeat. However, they had no choice. There was hardly any food left, the water was running out, and they did not know how long it would take until they met someone in this desolate land who could help them.

The remaining 29 men went further. At about 10 o'clock in the morning, they suddenly saw two people crossing the road they were following; two inhabitants of the country through which they were trying to find their way. Eyks gave a lively description of the event. 'We walked towards them, but they walked away. We kept on walking and discovered a camel at about 11 or 12 o'clock. We went towards it and then saw that the front legs of the animal were bound together. Four people came towards us straight away. It was their camel. As it seemed as if they did not dare to come closer, we stood close together in anticipation.'

Eyks thereupon sent two men to them, and some time later, the four of them came back with both men to the waiting group. 'But none of us could understand them. That is why we asked them how to get to Muscat. They did not understand that either, but they all called out together "Arabs! Arabs!," and they made it clear to us that, if we went further, our throats would be cut and we would be eaten, which — as Eyks said — was of little consolation to us.' Eyks continued: 'They asked us where we came from. We made it clear to them that our ship had run aground and we had swum to the shore. Afterwards we asked them for food and drink. But they showed that they did not have anything with them. At the last minute, however, they nevertheless gave us a bit of water from a leather pouch. The water looked reddish.'

Let us first take a moment to consider what Eyks says and how he presents the situation.

Eyks describes the situation from his point of view, using the first person plural and referring to 'we.' This is ambiguous: 'we' usually means 'we, the group of men,' or sometimes, 'Eyks and one or more others from the group' (for example Eyks and the boatswain). He sometimes uses the term 'we' in reference to himself, however, out of modesty (and thus avoids using the first person singular, or 'I'). The use of the first person plural means that the term 'they' refers to third parties, in this case, the inhabitants of the country. So, in encounters such as those described above, 'they' therefore means 'the others.' In confrontations with the inhabitants, 'they' are the opposing party. When the resulting sentence structures are too complicated, I have used direct quotes from the logbook, as above. In these quoted passages, however, the 18th-century language has been modernised somewhat to make his account more readable, as it is rather complex in this respect.

Next in his logbook, Eyks wrote something about the four people who had given them some water to drink. There were two women and two youths. The youths wore only a cloth round their lower bodies and a piece of goatskin on their heads. They had *assegais* and *khanjars* (*kromzwaarden* in contemporary Dutch; Eyks called them *buiksnijders*).[37]

'The women wore large cloths as garments, which extended from head to toe, and long trousers. Their hair was braided. While we stood there and asked them for help, they started plucking at our clothes. They tried to plunder us, but when we realised that, we left them and continued walking. They screamed at us and picked up stones to throw at us.'

At about 3 o'clock, three men with a camel came towards them. 'They behaved in a very friendly way, but we did not trust them. Our men asked them the way to Muscat, but they continuously shouted "Arabs! Arabs!" and made it clear to us that they[38] would behead us if we went further. We then asked them by way of gestures for food and drink, but did not get anything.'

One of the three men, an old fellow, sent the camel and both other men away to fetch water. 'He stayed with us and behaved in an ostensibly friendly way towards us. After sundown, we made ourselves ready to go to sleep. We looked sadly at one another, complained of hunger, thirst and stiffness and, lamenting, asked the Lord for a way out. Then seven camels arrived, mounted

---

37 Eyks defined them as follows: *assagaaien* are spears, *buiksnijders* are large, broad, crooked daggers.

38 This is an interpretation: these inhabitants might have meant that *they* would kill them if the men went further, because they had not given them anything in return for the precious water.

by nine men. All of the men sang and threw their spears high in the air and caught them, and came at us with naked backswords (*houwers* or *khanjars*) in their fists. They acted as if they wanted to eat us alive. They jumped off their camels and came at us. The old man walked towards them and acted as if he wanted to calm them down, but they slashed furiously at us and threw stones at us. Whereupon we too picked up stones and threw them at them as hard as we could. We drove them off by doing so. But they came back and threw a stone that made a hole right next to my eye. On that occasion, one of the seamen was slashed in the neck with a backsword. We wound a cloth around his neck and drove them off again. They left us in peace the rest of that night. The old fellow laughed about it and started gathering things to make a fire, but we stopped him because we did not trust him, and we kept a sharp watch. At night we put an old red cloak on him.' Eyks does not mention why they did that; possibly he was cold, or they may have given him the cloak to humour him, or perhaps even to keep a better eye on him.

'That night we heard the murmur of the sea in the distance.' Relieved, Eyks noted down that they must now be near the shore. The next day, it would become evident that the strategy of cutting through to the Gulf of Masirah by going straight across the desert in a north-easterly direction had been the right one. Seeing the sea again would not only cheer the men and put them at ease, but it was also proof that they had run aground on Cape Mataraca. Jonas Daalberg must have had the same idea. Eyks, however, did not mention anything about this in his logbook, nor did he do so elsewhere in his text.

Along the Gulf of Masirah

The party moved on as soon as it became light, but one of the soldiers lay down and did not get up again. He said he could no longer keep up with the group, and would rather stay there and wait for death. They then arrived at a high, rocky mountain range that extended along the coast, but it was so steep that they could not climb down anywhere. At this point, Eyks continues his account with evident relief: 'Here both of the men who were sent away with two camels the day before came towards us with six jugs of water in a leather bag, enough to allow each of us to drink something. It did us good to moisten our tongues again.

After both men had spoken to the old man, they made it clear to us that they would give us more water and also food, if we laid everything we had on their camels. We did so and also mounted one of the European men and the black boy. They then started plucking at our clothes and touching our bodies. Two women also arrived, each with a baby in a cradle on her back. The cradles were

26 – Steep cliffs in the south of the Gulf of Masirah. Area c. 3,7 × 5,2 km, eye level 5,4 km.

made of twigs bound together, and were fastened around their necks with rope. Both women also shook and plucked at us, just like the men. We did not like that, and we demanded that they stop. Then they wanted to leave with their camels, but the old man did not allow that. It seemed, however, that the women were in charge there, because they took their camels with them. We went further with our gear on our backs again, towards the seaward side. Together with the men, they seemed to be in the mood for a fight with stones, but they were afraid we would be too strong. They confined themselves to watching us for a while.'

What can we make of this very first encounter with the Bedouin? Eyks and his men apparently did not appreciate having their belongings and clothes plucked at in this manner. He described that behaviour as 'plundering' and may have assumed that they wanted to take everything away from them. The day before, however, the women had given precious water to a party of strange, thirsty men, who had all kinds of things with them. Something had to be given in return. They were out to barter; to trade to their advantage. The misunderstanding was not resolved because they did not understand each other. The ritual was repeated after both men had tested their willingness to barter with six jugs of water. Things went wrong, however, not because the seamen did not want to exchange anything, but because they did not appreciate the Bedouin's interest in their clothes and the rest of their possessions; an interest which, in their view, was impertinent. They feared they would be robbed. Their superior numbers, however, prevented this from turning into a violent confrontation.

They trekked further. After some time, they arrived at a place in the mountains that seemed to promise water, but they failed to find any. Only after they had walked back and forth on the cliff for a long time did they find both a well with brackish water and a cormorant close to the coast, for which they thanked the Lord together. They killed the cormorant, skinned it and ate and drank what they had with relish. They stayed where they were for that day and the following night. The next morning, when they had filled their empty kegs and jugs, six of the men wanted to stay there, but were persuaded with encouraging words to go along with the others.

Hunger, thirst, rocks and robbers

TUESDAY, 16 AUGUST

The men continued their journey at sunrise. It took them up and down the mountains, as it was not possible to avoid them by walking along the coast. At about 11 o'clock or 12 noon they saw a thorn tree that promised some shade, and they all sat down under it together. The sun was so terribly bright that most of them nearly fainted from the heat.

'At about 2 o'clock, nine camels with people came towards us. They sang, threw their *assegais* in the air and acted as if they wanted to eat us alive. When they were close to us, they made it clear with gestures that they wanted to cut off our heads. They threw an *assegai* towards us, so we picked up stones and threw them at the people, which drove them away time after time and made them flee. Then some men in our group decided to take their camels from them. One of them, however, was keeping watch over the animals and got them running. One could be caught nevertheless. We wanted to cut its throat, but the animal escaped from us.'

Eyks was worried about the situation. Although the Bedouin were in the minority, they had weapons and did not hesitate to attack. Killing a camel would undoubtedly have escalated the conflict. His logbook shows that he was very alert and chose his words carefully. Eyks described the nine Bedouin as a 'gang' — a word that, in his day, did not always have the negative connotations it has today. It might just have been his way of describing 'a threatening group with unclear intentions,' even though these intentions appeared malicious.

The logbook then continues: 'In this gang were the two men who had tried to kidnap[39] us the day before on the camels, and they were the very ones who fought most bitterly and the longest against us, from half-past two in the afternoon until after sundown, and they still did not want to give up.'

Their water ran out in the afternoon. Many of the men were ill and could not keep up any longer. 'Therefore we decided to try something: we wanted to try and find out what they actually wanted. We took a pair of trousers, a shirt and some other togs, stuffed them into a pillowcase and threw it to them. Then

39 This is the most likely interpretation of Eyks' meaning here, although it is remarkable that such an intention cannot be derived from his account of the day before.

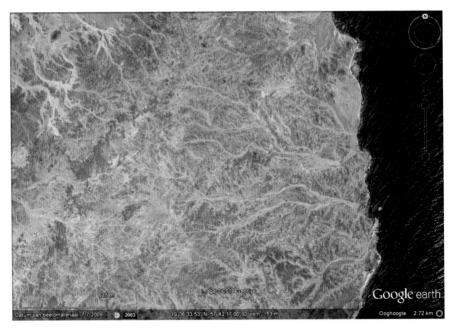

27 – Nothing all day long but high, rocky land and dry valleys... Area c. 1,9 × 2,8 km, eye level 2,7 km.

they indicated that we could go further.' A solution had been found, and the balance was restored. The men on the camels accepted the clothes in the pillowcase as the conclusion of the previous day's interrupted barter session, and were able to go back to where they had come from with their heads held high.

Eyks and the boatswain took stock of the injuries. Four men had been injured in the skirmish, and their wounds were bound as well as could be managed. They set out immediately afterwards, and walked almost all night long. Meanwhile, many complained of hunger and thirst and stiffness in their loins, because it was sweltering hot during the day and bitterly cold at night in the open air.

WEDNESDAY, 17 AUGUST

At daybreak, after a short night with little sleep, the men went farther. They searched for water all day long, but did not find any. They were thus forced to drink their own water (urine) and salt water. Two seamen[40] were unable to continue because of thirst. Eyks confined himself to stating this as a fact in his logbook, although the situation must have affected him deeply. Those who were able had to move on as quickly as possible, however; after all, one cannot last very long on urine and salt water.

40 One of them was Steven Hillekens, who gave his account to Eyks on 13 December 1763.

28 – A rocky coast with some flamingos and possibly also the 'marsh samphire' that had so disagreed with them.

They saw nothing all day long but high, rocky land and dry valleys, and looked dejectedly at each other. In their prayers, each man begged the Lord in his heart for a way out or, if it should please Him, to deliver him from this miserable life by letting him die. Only 26 men were left in the group of men who again lay down to rest at sundown.

THURSDAY, 18 AUGUST

The men moved on again at daybreak. Their search for water revealed nothing but salt water, with which they attempted to quench their thirst insofar as this was possible. Along the way, they ate green herbs that somewhat resembled marsh samphire.[41] These plants had a briny, bitter taste, and it gave most of them diarrhoea, which weakened them even more.

'Then the boatswain's mate, Pieter van Holland, and a seaman, Carsten Pieters-ze, remained behind in the mountains.' This time Eyks did note the names of those who stayed behind, but he said nothing about the gravity of their condition or the reason for their decision. Did the event affect him? Together with a seaman, Pieter van Holland had saved Eyks from certain death by drowning by cutting his heavy, drenched tailcoat from his body just in time. Did Eyks not

41 Marsh samphire: a tasty plant growing on sandy flats on the West Frisian islands and in Zeeland.

say more about them because he had come to know both men well, and their giving up — of all people — disappointed or deeply touched him? Or was there another reason for his silence? The logbook does not give a conclusive answer at this stage, and only later does it become clear what had happened.

Trapped by the Bedouin

The group was now down to 24 men. At about 3 o'clock in the afternoon, they arrived at a level seashore with swampy ground. They found a boat that had been smashed to pieces on the shore, a cotton fishing net in the sand and a large empty jug. At about 5 o'clock, they saw the same people again coming towards them with their camels.

'We were able to offer little or no resistance, not only because there were no stones on that swampy ground, but also because we were exhausted and it did not matter much to us if they took our lives. It would have been a more attractive prospect to die, if that was God's will. While walking, however, we found some stones which enabled us to offer some resistance and not surrender to that gang of robbers straight away.'

They did not give up without a fight. 'However, when we had no more stones left, we had to give up. They came at us furiously. They put their naked back-swords on our stomachs or chests, and their crooked daggers on our throats, and forced us to take off our clothes, except for a few pairs of trousers. Anyone who did not do so fast enough had his clothes cut off his body. We now looked at each other with tear-filled eyes and began to groan, but they laughed at that. Nonetheless, it pleased the Lord to soften their hearts somewhat. They gave us back our empty kegs and jugs, and then one received a shirt, the other a smock, yet another a sleeveless undershirt and so forth. Afterwards, they gestured that we could leave, but they still threw a few stones at us six times as a farewell.'

The Bedouin knew the area and had followed an effective strategy to corner the group without endangering themselves. There were no stones on the swampy ground, which was perhaps a lagoon. Eyks' men were unable to defend themselves there. The Bedouin attacked the defenceless, exhausted seamen without wounding them and took from them what they wanted. No wonder the men were near desperation; they could not find any water, and still had so far to go.

At a forked river (near Duqm)

Trekking farther, the men arrived at a fork in a large river that flowed out to the sea. They walked some way inland, searching for a place where they could wade to the other side. They eventually crossed with the water up to their necks. All managed to reach the other side, except for the little Javanese boy, whom Eyks usually called the Slave Boy. He was initially swept away seawards and almost drowned, but fortunately he, too, managed to reach the other side. They probably drank the seaward-flowing water, because that evening they continued to walk until about 10 o'clock, and only then did they lie down to rest. They covered themselves with sand before going to sleep.

Eyks ended his account of this oppressive day with a heartfelt lament: 'Up to now, we have not been able to sense that the people we have met live in houses somewhere inland, or practise any religion, or do any work besides robbing and stealing, which is accursed work.'

Eyks was clearly fed up at this point. Six men had already dropped out of the group; thirst, hunger and exhaustion had taken their toll; the little Javanese boy had only narrowly escaped death that very day. There was only one way out: in a last desperate effort, they would have to keep up the pace. Eyks realised that they had a long way to go, although he may not have realised quite how far; they had travelled less than a quarter of the distance to Ras al Hadd, the known cape in the north.

Where on earth were they? Remarkably enough, Eyks' mentioning of the wide forked river in his logbook played a vital role in the search for the location of the wreck of the *Amstelveen*. On the basis of the nautical information in the logbook, it could not initially be determined with certainty where the ship was lost. Somewhere on the stretch of beach running from east to west, to the west of Masirah? Or in the northern part of the Bay of Sawqirah, at Cape Madrakah (Cape Mataraca)?

Initially I, just like Eyks in the early morning of 6 August, concluded that the ship had probably run aground somewhere in the Gulf of Masirah. In that case, the men must have walked about 250 km along the hot beach scattered with high cliffs [rock masses]. Eyks' account of the walk, however, gives a totally different picture of the landscape through which they trekked. No river, for instance, could be seen there that branched out to the sea. At that time, how-

29 – The old, generally dry forked riverbeds near Duqm. Near the coast water is flooding in during the rising tide. The sea is just yet visible top right. This image was captured on 07-07-2009. Area c. 1,9 × 2,8 km, eye level 2,7 km.

ever, I had yet to discover the letters written by Eyks and Buschman about the accident. Only after I had consulted these letters in the VOC Archives did it first occur to me that Cape Mataraca might be the location of the shipwreck.

At first, I was unable to believe it: after all, if that had been the case, the

30 – Barefoot over sharp rocks and hot sand in suffocating heat, day after day, with neither water nor hardly any food...

[67]

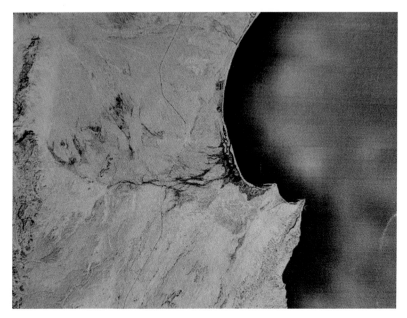

31 – The forked riverbeds near Duqm where the Javanese boy almost drowned in August 1763. This crucial satellite image (in b/w) was captured on 19-12-2003 and derived from the internet early 2009. It has been substituted in a recent update by Google Earth.

survivors would have had to walk more than 500 km to arrive in Hadd. To me, this seemed absolutely impossible: to walk barefoot over sharp rocks and hot sand in suffocating heat, day after day, with no water and hardly any food. A simple realisation put me on the right track. The walk must have started at the wreck. If the journey could be traced from the start, the dilemma of the wreck's location would be solved at the same time.

Using Google Earth, I scanned the south coast and eventually found two old riverbeds near Duqm. It was possible to quickly survey the different landscapes through which the survivors had trekked. The sequence of those landscape elements was essential, and the result was correct, down to the minutest detail. They started their journey at Cape Mataraca.

It might seem unbelievable, but it is true. Duqm is located over at least 100 km, as the crow flies, from the place where they ran aground. Including all of the interruptions, they covered that distance in slightly over a week. Incredibly, using Google Earth in the comfort of one's own home, one can now follow in the men's footsteps, and trace a journey that was made 250 years ago — a challenge that is certainly worth the effort!

Saved by some water

At sunrise — thus a bit later than before — the men were on the road again, although 'many of our company said that they could not keep up with us anymore and they would rather die here, because they were going to die of thirst anyway.' Nevertheless, by talking to them and encouraging them, Eyks and the boatswain were able to persuade the men to come along. This compliance did not last long, however, because at about 10 o'clock, the assistant cook, Hans Lutjes, and a seaman succumbed to thirst and refused to go further. Now down to 22 men, they went on until about 11 o'clock. They all became ill as a result of the unbearable heat and thirst, and could go no further. Having sat down for some time, the men nevertheless got back on their feet to go further and search for water. However, they were unable to rouse the bay man, Pieter Coene, and a junior seaman named Bronkhorst. Thirst prevented them from going further. Eyks must have been particularly affected by the bay man's predicament. Both men came from Middelburg and had spent a lot of time together since they left the beach near to the wreck. He realised that his townsman would not make it without water and would have to die there.

He wrote in his logbook that it seemed that it would have been 'everyone's turn' if not the Lord, who has a remedy against death, had saved them. 'He, however, showed us his mercy and once again gave us water to revive us, with which we could refresh our thirsty insides. At about noon, we found a small pool 4 or 5 feet long and 1.5 inches deep and saw, to our amazement, how the water continued to surge up out of the ground. Here I remembered what is written in Isaiah XLI: 17, 18: *"When the poor and needy seek water, and there is none, and their tongue faileth for thirst, I the Lord will hear them, I the God of Israel will not forsake them. I will open rivers in high places, and fountains in the midst of the valleys: I will make the wilderness a pool of water, and the dry land springs of water."*

'We fell on our knees and drank so much water that we spat out the salt water we had drunk two days long. We then found a pool of water that was larger, with a large thorn tree standing next to it. We thanked the Lord for his mercy and rested there that day. We then looked for food, but found only thin rushes from which we sucked the juice from the roots. We finally filled our kegs and jugs and sent a soldier with a stoup[42] full of water to the bay man and the

---

42 Stoup — a jug holding approximately 2 litres.

junior seaman, who had remained lying at a distance of approximately 1 mile [7.4 km] from us. The soldier found the two men and brought them back to us. So we 22 persons were together again.'

They also found several graves there.[43] A jar or piece of wood or fishing net had been placed at each grave. They stayed there until the next morning.

SATURDAY, 20 AUGUST

The party travelled farther at sunrise, but not long afterwards they were attacked again by some men and women, who pulled the full kegs and jugs out of their hands and robbed them of everything they still had,[44] meanwhile threatening to cut their throats. Eyks made it clear to them that they could just go ahead, as they had stripped them naked and taken away their water. Now they simply had to put an end to their lives. The men would have to die of thirst or the sun would burn their bodies, it was so hot. Their appeals were met with laughter. The men looked dejectedly at one another and some began to weep. 'When they saw that, they gave us a drink of water from our own casks and made it clear that we could now leave. But when we asked for our property back, an old, ailing man walked towards us. He looked at us for a while and then gave us some casks back, which were now almost empty. He also gave one of us a pair of trousers, another a smock, and yet another a pair of trousers or a sleeveless frock. Some, however, did not get anything and had to go on naked.'

The men divided these things among them, so that they could at any rate cover the lower parts of their bodies. Eyks got crimp's[45] trousers and half a leg of seaman's trousers to hang across his shoulders. Everyone was roasted that day by the burning sun. While on their way, they saw some oryx[46] for the first time. Walking across the rocks caused painful wounds to develop on the soles of their feet, leaving them barely able to move. They went to sleep after sundown.

SUNDAY, 21 AUGUST

At sunrise, the men went farther. They trekked through high mountains with deep valleys, but did not find any water. Eventually, they arrived back on the beach, where they found crabs and winkles. They also ate a sort of root that

43 Eyks wrote: *begraafplaatsen* (graveyards). The context shows that he meant a few graves.
44 Eyks wrote: *moedernaakt uitschudden* ('fleeced them stark-naked'). So the men and women also stole the clothing they still had on.
45 Crimp (*zielverkoper* in Dutch) — someone who press-ganged seamen using illegal practices. *Ziel* is a corruption of *ceel* (loan note); crimps were often women.
46 Eyks wrote *bokken*. These were possibly Arabian oryx: white, longhorn gemsboks, hunted to extinction, but returned to the wild from zoos. These splendid animals nowadays live in protected desert reserves. Recently their numbers have fallen again due to illegal hunting.

resembled the crown of a pineapple. The root tasted sweet, but had a bitter aftertaste. They saw boats on the beach, made in the same way as the sewn boats on the coast of Coromandel. There they also found the heads and fins of sharks, on which they gnawed. Most of the men had been burnt severely by the hot sun, and they all had blisters on the soles of their feet from walking on the stones. Many complained of pain and wanted to remain lying there. After sundown, they rested again, but did not get much sleep because of the cold.

MONDAY, 22 AUGUST

The boatswain and Eyks had great difficulty in convincing many of the men to go further, but they eventually persuaded everyone to join them. The men had to scramble up and down the cliffs, onto which the waves were crashing. The high crags were too steep: it was impossible to climb them. They had no choice; they had to clamber over the rocks on the shore to make any progress at all. This was very difficult, and resulted in a lot of sore feet.

Quite soon, two men lay down and were unable to go farther. One seaman, named Jan Drevan, was in a serious condition. His limbs had become stiff, he had contracted lockjaw (and therefore could not talk), and he was suffering from two severely painful fingers that had previously been partially amputated. The other was the junior seaman, Bronkhorst, who had been brought back before by a soldier. Both were left to their fate, like the other men who had given up. Nothing more could be done for them.

The group went farther and arrived at a sandy beach. There they found the boatswain's mate, Pieter van Holland, whom they had lost in the mountains on 18 August. He was sitting in the sand, wearing nothing but a smock. Next to him sat a seaman, Jacob Kleyn, who had stayed behind on 17 August because of thirst. He wore only a small loincloth. They said that they, too, had to hand over all their clothing and that the seaman, Carsten Pietersze, had gone on ahead.

Eyks noted down who had given up that day, but he also described how they would now and again encounter men who had fallen behind. These men sometimes re-joined the group. He did not, however, do so systematically in a way that gave a clear picture. A few personal details are known of just 19 of the 30 men who started on the journey. It must have been a relief to Eyks that some of the men who had given up during the journey had gone farther on their own.

The fate of the little Javanese boy

He then saw some men with fishing gear coming towards them. 'They asked where we came from. We made it clear that we had swum to the shore. They then asked how come our bodies looked so terribly battered. We showed them that we had been burnt by the sun. They then asked whether we had brought any clothes to shore, and if we had any *floes* [money, gold or silver]. They finally winked to indicate that we could go along with them.

'We followed them, and soon arrived at their dwelling: a thorn tree in the flat field. That is where they kept women, children, camels, donkeys, billy goats and dogs. Their household effects amounted to a pot, *lokjes* (wooden boxes) and oyster shells. Their women looked compassionately at us, showing clearly that they took pity on us, and lamented that we looked so awful. They asked us all kinds of questions and then invited us to eat with them, despite their poverty. They gave us a roasted shark fin, a piece of dried shark and each of us a piece of *tamr*.'

32 – Camels with their offspring, resting but watchful.

Dates? Did Eyks not know of these fruits? At this point, he considered it necessary to insert an explanation in his logbook: 'a type of fruit that grows here and is about the size of and tastes like a fig. They are oval-shaped and have a stone the size of a coffee bean on the inside.' He probably did not know the word 'date': he always wrote *tammer* (i.e. *tamr*), which means both 'date(s)' and 'a lump of sticky dates.'

This was their first meal since 15 August. The women milked the goats and gave them the milk, mixed with water, to drink. They also gave pieces of cloth to two men to cover their nakedness. The women showed that they would very much like to have the little slave boy, but Eyks did not want to relinquish him to them. Daalberg was of the same mind. Immediately afterwards, they were told that they had to leave. The men asked how long it would take to get to Muscat, and were told that it was still very far away. They kept on walking until sundown, and then went to sleep.

TUESDAY, 23 AUGUST

The men set out again the next morning. Suddenly, they noticed that a man on a camel was following them. They recognised the man as one of those who had been at the thorn tree the day before. When he caught up with them, he made it clear that he wanted to take the Javanese boy from them. His request was refused, but he was not deterred. 'He gestured that if we went on without giving him the boy, our heads would be cut off. We then made it clear to him that he could take the boy if he consented and wanted to go with him. He took the boy nevertheless against his will, rode to two other men and handed the boy to them. Then he came back and brought us a small basket of *tamr*. We walked further, but after some time, four seamen of our company remained lying down.'

Eyks did not record which of the four seamen suddenly stayed behind, or why they did so. After all, they had all eaten and drunk the day before. It seems that the hopeless journey in the heat was too much for them.

The men finally arrived at a grove where they got some water, but they had to drink it out of their hands and therefore spilled a lot of the precious liquid. Everyone thought this a pity, but Eyks took it particularly to heart.

In the meantime, many seamen began to moan and to curse. This, too, irritated Eyks. He had already discussed the issue with the boatswain; it was clear that the men were fed up with trudging, and had no idea when the hopeless situation would end. The men became indifferent, and showed their dissatisfaction 'as if they wanted to put God in his place, which is very much human nature.'

Shaken, Eyks addressed the men and asked them if they perhaps knew a shorter way than he and the boatswain. He told them that if so, they should take it, because he could not stop them, as he was too weak to even bear his own body. He added that he and the boatswain would no longer beg them to set off somewhat earlier in the morning and continue an hour longer in the evening, something they had already done several times.

Immediately afterwards, Eyks and Daalberg decided to speed up their journey. They said that whoever wanted could come with them, but that they had to realise that the entire journey was a matter of guesswork; because, as Eyks wrote, 'We did not have a compass and therefore had no guideline other than walking so that the sun stayed to the right of us.'

This is the first and only passage in the logbook where Eyks sets out his strategy, and also the only time he expresses his irritation and disappointment. The journey demanded the utmost from everyone, also from him. It was cool early in the morning. If they got up earlier and went on a few hours longer after sundown, they would be able to gain a lot of distance. They had to achieve a substantial distance each day. Their perilous situation forced them to hurry to have any chance of completing this seemingly impossible journey. The moaning and cursing had deeply affected Eyks. He only wanted the best for his men, and there was no other likely way out of the misery than to keep on walking along the shore.

At sundown, the men tried to sleep, but got little rest because it was so cold at night.

A warmer welcome

In the morning, the men went on further again. Eyks gave no indication of how late they set off or how big the group was. After some time, they encountered some 'Blacks'[47] who gave them water and *tamr*. They also filled their casks and jugs with water. The men were asked once again if they had *floes* and *groo-sie*[48] (silver and gold) on them, where they came from, and why their bodies looked so awful. Eyks understood their questions, but could only answer with gestures. He made it clear that their bodies had been burnt by the sun and then heard that in their language, the sun is called '*sjemes*' [shams]. They also asked why their feet looked so battered. The men showed them the soles of their feet and then they understood that the wounds had been caused by stones and hot sand. But they did not seem to comprehend the cause of these injuries, pointing to their own bodies and feet. Apparently they were wondering why they did not also look so pitiful. Finally Eyks concluded: 'Nevertheless, they seemed to feel sorry for us, because they gave us three big raw shark fins as a gift.'

The group went further and came to a large plain. Eyks, Daalberg and Pieter Coene, the bay man, then walked in a straight line across the plain to avoid a big sand bar. The rest of the men walked along the beach. Eyks wrote: 'We had passed the plain after sundown and went to sleep under a cliff. The others joined us later. Then we heard two Blacks whom we asked for some fire. They gestured to us that a few men from our group should go with them to their abode. This proved also to be a cliff, just like our resting place, but they did not find any fire. So we had to eat the shark fins raw.'

They also found Carsten Pietersze there, the seaman who had left the group on 18 August. Serious sunburn had left him barely recognisable. He maintained that it was better to travel in groups of two or four men than in a large party.

Was this the reason why more and more seamen stayed behind and continued on their way at their own pace? Did they realise how dangerous this was?

---

47 Coastal residents, problaby of East African origin. Eyks called them *Zwarten* (black people). 'Throughout history people from a large variety of ethnic, cultural and religious backgrounds have settled in the region.' (C.W. Hoek, 1998, p. 58).

48 *Floes* [flu:s] and *groosie* (Arab. gorooshi) (from: Groschen) are coins (silver, gold).

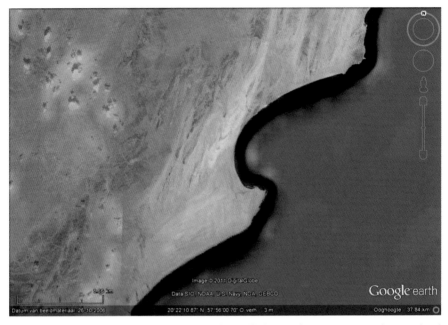

33 – Huge sand flat along the north coast of the Gulf of Masirah. Area c. 25 × 41 km, eye level 38 km.

Up until then, they had always been in the majority in confrontations with Bedouin; travelling in larger numbers made them relatively safe. On the other hand, it was always difficult for a large group of men to find enough food and drink for everyone. The fishermen were also poor, and naturally did not appreciate having so many guests at once. It was a difficult dilemma.

THURSDAY, 25 AUGUST
'The boatswain, the bay man and I each put a stoup of water on our shoulder and continued on our way.'

Had events taken a spectacular turn?

At first, still on the beach near the wreck, Eyks started his logbook with a seamanlike account of the weather and wind. After a few days of wandering in the desert, he started each new entry with a variation on the miracle of each day: the dawn, the return of the light, the rising of the sun. Following on from that, he noted how the group started travelling that particular day.

This day, however, Eyks started with a completely different opening sentence: an announcement of a major change, in a curt and decisive tone. What is more, for the first time during the journey, Eyks adopted the first person singular ('I'). His statement implicitly suggested that the knot had finally been cut. The three men decided to continue their journey together and to move on more quickly. Eyks does not tell us who had cut the knot and what the exact reason for this was, but one can speculate all the same. In their opinion, the

34 – Shortcut through the Wahibi Sands in NE direction to the coast (a beach) north of Masirah Island (that they didn't see). Area c. 90 × 140 km, eye level 125 km.

group was not progressing fast enough. Two days after Eyks's warning, he told the men that each would henceforth go their own way. Anyone who wanted could come along, and for those who did not, Eyks had made his strategy clear: keep the sun to the right and keep on walking for as long as possible.

None of the men joined Eyks and his companions. Does this suggest that Eyks had previously demanded too much of them? But the boatswain also chose to hurry and let the seamen go their own way from then on. The surgeon's second mate apparently had the same idea. Both men had confidence in Eyks. The group had now definitely split up, but did they actually know where they were? Eyks and Daalberg realised that their location would become clear over the next few days, and that they should reach the long shore towards Ras al Hadd, the well-known cape in the north, but they had no idea of the terrain that still awaited them.

The route first took them along the seashore, as it had done over the last few days. Eyks noted that, 'We met two inhabitants who took us along to their home under a cliff. They asked the same questions as the last ones. They eventually gave us water and a piece of grilled fish. The seamen De Geus,[49] Andries Kolstrop and Jacobus Balthazar joined us here. The six of us thus went onwards. We soon met four men who had five loaded camels with them. We asked them

49 Possibly *Cornelis de Reus*, a boatswain's mate; Eyks did not mention his first name.

35 – Edge of a wood of prosopis trees in soft sandy ground.

the way to Muscat, and they made it clear with gestures that we still had seven days' travel to go. They told us which paths we had to take; these were three or four frequently-used paths. We walked farther on these paths, hoping that the Lord would give us a way out if it pleased Him.

Towards the evening, we came to a fresh-water creek, where we refreshed ourselves and refilled both our jugs. From there, we arrived at a wood in sandy ground. This felt good on our feet and gave us new courage, but we lost our way in the sand. Nevertheless, we walked a bit further into the wood. After sundown we went to sleep, but our night's sleep was interrupted by the cold and the pain we felt in our burnt bodies.'

Through the high sand dunes

FRIDAY, 26 AUGUST

At daybreak, the six men went further through the wood, which was approximately two to three German miles (15–22 km) long. They ended up in exceptionally high sand dunes, and had to walk through the loose, hot sand on their bruised feet. This was both difficult and very painful. In the evening, at about 10 o'clock, the men went to sleep. They dug themselves into the sand so that only their faces were exposed, but the cold of the night prevented them from getting much rest.

SATURDAY, 27 AUGUST

When morning came, the men went further. Along the way they dug for water, but found only salt water. They thought that they would die of thirst in those high sand dunes, and suffered dreadfully from the heat. They made it till the evening, however, and went to sleep, just like the day before.

36 – They ended up in exceptionally high sand dunes...

The six men set out again in the morning, but they had a lot of trouble persuading the bay man, Pieter Coene, to come along. He was the most sunburnt of them all. Under way, they dug a well and found fresh water, with which they refreshed themselves and filled their jugs. At about 4 o'clock they arrived at a beach, where they sat down in the wet sand to rest a while. Then three men came towards them with a loaded camel. The cargo consisted of bags of fish (they looked like sardines), bags of *tamr* and bags of dried limes. They were unable to find out where the cargo was being taken, because they could not understand the men. The men were dressed only in goatskins round their bodies, and were otherwise totally naked.

Eyks summarised the encounter as follows: 'We asked for some food. They gave us a piece of date cake and tried to find out where we came from and so forth. Afterwards, they searched us and felt the waistbands of our trousers to see if we had money on us, but because they did not find anything, they left us. After this, we met two other men. They took us close to their lodging, which was made of thorny branches in the shape of a half-moon as protection against the wind. This was the first building[50] we had seen in this country. We were given a piece of *tamr* here, too, and continued walking until after sundown. Then we lay down on the beach to rest. Two jackals came at night, which frightened us, but they fled from us on their own.'

The six men – Eyks, the boatswain, the bay man and the three seamen who had joined them – had lived through four trying days. They had cut through a wood and trekked across the high sizzling-hot sand dunes to the shore. There, they had encountered a different sort of people; men who apparently fished for a living, who also grew fruit and had date palms; or market gardeners who also fished. These men clearly took their merchandise somewhere, perhaps to merchants or to a market in the surroundings. The structure that protected them from the wind shows that these were people with a more or less permanent abode.

Where, exactly, had the six men ended up, and were they making faster progress now that they had split from the other group? From the river near Duqm (18 August) they had walked northwards past a sand bar (probably Ras Bintawt) in the northwest of the Gulf of Masirah (24 August). This was a difficult journey across rocks, roughly 100 km as the crow flies, which took six days. The next day, Eyks, Daalberg and Coene went farther along the coast and through a wood with a creek (perhaps a tributary of the Wadi Halfain). Afterwards, they trudged across high, sizzling-hot sand dunes *(the Wahiba or Sharqiyah Sands)*

---

50 A man-made structure for protection against the wind, indicating semi-permanent occupation.

and reached a beach in the afternoon. In a straight line, this was also a journey of at least 100 km, completed in barely four days. It was good that it had not lasted much longer, however, difficult as it was. The six men had indeed travelled faster in a smaller group. Yet, the two routes differed substantially and they had encountered less trouble from native inhabitants out for barter or robbery.

AN AMAZING VARIATION OF LANDSCAPES

'The landscape of al-Sharqiyah is varied; mountaineous in the north-east and a preponderance of gravel plains in most other parts, with thorn and dry savannah vegetation, interspersed with limestone and ophiolite hill ranges rising some 150 feet above the plains. The sand desert (Eastern Sands) forms the central and southern part of the region. This area is covered by linear dunes of several tens of kilometers in length, some of which reach a height of more than 300 meters. The vegetation of the desert and its margins is scanty with the exception of parts of the eastern and south-western edge which are covered with relatively dense woodlands of prosopis trees. Salt flats cover part of the coastal area and the southern edge of the Eastern Sands, which are almost destitute of vegetation. The sandy and rocky beaches carved out in the limestones and aeolionites that cover part of the southern coast line offer space for fishing activities. The region is crossed by two main wadi courses, with numerous tributaries. They run along either sides of the Sands; the north-eastern one, named Wadi Batha for a large part of its course, drains into the Arabian Sea near al-Ashkharah and the western one which has two main courses, Wadi Andam (with Wadi Halfayn) and Wadi Matam, drains into the Bay of Mahawt. Most oases settlements are distributed along these wadi courses. The climate is typical for the (semi-) arid zone: the average yearly temperature is about 30 degrees Celsius with a maximum of over 50 degrees Celsius. Precipitation is below 150 mm a year. Rainfall occurs mainly in winter and occasional torrential rains cause floods and landslides. During summer, easterly and south-easterly winds bring dust and sandstorms to the inland areas. These same winds bring coolness to the coastal areas, and cause the sea to be rough during this period. The climate and weather contribute to unpredictable living conditions to which the inhabitants have been able to adapt during the course of time, making a sustainable living for themselves.

(–)

The coast, the Sands and the mountainous areas are difficult to access. Tracks in the coastal areas, for example, are regularly blocked by dunes blown over from the Sands. The coastal villages are linked by a metalled road from Ras al-Ruways to al-Ashkharah. This route extends southwards as a dirt road into the area where sand spurs reach the Arabian Sea. In this part of the Sands the tracks disappear in *high dunes, where only skilled drivers (such as Bedouin fish traders) can find their way across.'*

C.W. Hoek, Shifting Sands, *1998, p. 58–59.*

Between 1987 and 1998 Corien Hoek, a Dutch anthropologist, carried out field research in Sharqiyah: the region north of the Gulf of Masirah where during their trek in 1763 Eyks and his companions struggled to reach Ras Al Hadd.

Encounters on the Sharqiyah coast

The six men continued their journey at daybreak, but they again had great difficulty in persuading Pieter Coene to join them. Shortly after setting out, they came across two boats in which seven black men were sitting. These men questioned them, as the others had done before. They also met two seamen, Matthys Janszen and Jan Theunisze. The latter had a large wound in the back of his heel, and had to walk with a stick. They told Eyks that they had lost sight of the others in the wood (the same wood to which Eyks refers on 25 August). Janzen and Theunisze continued onwards, joined by one of the seamen in Eyks' group, Jacob Johan Balthazar. Meanwhile, the bay man, Pieter Coene, and the boatswain, Jonas Daalberg, complained constantly because they had been terribly burnt by the sun, especially Coene.

In the course of the day, they came upon some huts, which were made of sticks and covered with goat-hair sacks. There was also a stone building nearby, which had been roughly built in the shape of a square: it looked as if paving stones and rocks had been laid on top of each other. This was the first time they encountered such a dwelling in this desolate, unpopulated country. Up until now, the only features in the landscape had been the occasional thorn tree and few other trees.[51] 'The people who lived here again asked us the usual questions, and searched us. They even pulled the cloth buttons off my trousers to see if money was concealed in them. More and more men and women came, and they asked us if we were circumcised. We did not understand why they came to us and opened our trousers. They used sticks to search our bodies[52] to see if we were circumcised. They did this several times and spat in our faces.' Eyks thought they were of Jewish or Turkish origin, because both peoples practised circumcision. Afterwards, they were nonetheless given some *tamr* and a few sips of water. They then left quickly, and went to sleep after sundown.

The men set off again at daybreak. On the way, they were frequently stopped, body searched and spat upon. Eventually, they came upon four men who had

---

51 Eyks forgot to mention the only exception: the wood with the soft sand and the creek.
52 Eyks used the word *visiteren* to mean both 'search' and 'body search'. It is not always clear further on in his account exactly which form he intended.

37 – Huts made of sticks of prosopis trees (in front).

caught a lot of fish, and Eyks asked them for some food. 'They indicated that we should go with them. We did so, and soon arrived at their huts. Their women felt sorry for us and promised to give us something to eat. They gave us fried fish, *tamr* and water, as much as we wanted. They even enjoyed watching us eat, because we ate with such gusto. It was a great boon that they were so generous in giving us food. That evening, we again found compassionate people. They welcomed us in the same way, but the bay man did not eat anything, although they did urge him to eat something. But he had pain everywhere and felt ill.

'Then they laid a large fishing net (a trawl- or dragnet) on the ground, in which we could sleep. I then said to Pieter Coene that, if I were ill, I would stay four days or so with these kind people, but he did not answer.'

WEDNESDAY, 31 AUGUST

The men left again in the morning. Pieter Coene took leave of the others at about 7 o'clock, saying that he would try to return to the huts, following the advice that Eyks had given him the night before. Walking on, they came upon some simply-made huts: they consisted of four stakes in the ground, 4 to 5 feet high, and were covered on top with camel-hair rugs. 'There we were asked again if we were circumcised. They searched our bodies as well and asked us if we wanted to stay there and have women. Others had already asked us that several times, but we did not answer and went further until the evening. Then we lay down and went to sleep.'

In the morning, the men trekked further, receiving a piece of *tamr* and some water on their way. In the afternoon, they found two seamen, Willem Nicolson and Carsten Pietersze, who were sitting on the beach eating a crab. Eyks: 'We thought at first that they were Blacks, but when we came closer, we saw that they were two of our own men. They told us that they had lost the others in the large wood and that a soldier,[53] who was still with them at the time, had later returned to the creek, saying that he wanted to die there. They also told us that they had visited our surgeon's second mate last night. Pieter Coene was in a very bad way, and they thought it unlikely that he would live much longer.'

Afterwards, each went his own way. Towards evening, Eyks' party came upon huts, where they asked for and received food and drink from the occupants. They were questioned again, but the people seemed highly sympathetic to the men's predicament. 'When they saw that my lips and those of the boatswain were very raw and grazed, they took a piece of black substance[54] which they moistened with water and rubbed on a piece of stone, and then smeared the mixture on our lips with a spatula. Both other seamen joined us again, and we stayed together from then on.

'In the evening, we gathered some twigs and clumps of grass to make some protection against the wind, and went to sleep behind it.'

At daybreak, the men continued their journey. They begged for some food and drink at some huts along the way, but were given nothing. Yet an old woman was willing to take them to a well. While they were going with her, the boatswain said that he could not move any more, and that he would lie there for about three days to see if his burnt body recovered. Eyks and the others went with the old woman to the well; a journey that took quite a lot of effort, as the well was located pretty far away and they had to walk across hot sand. The worst thing was that they were followed by boys and girls, who threw stones and teased them. They did not reach the well until about 11 or 12 o'clock. They found a man sitting there. 'The boys and girls gestured that he would behead us, but after questioning and searching us, he did not do so, but gave us a drink of water. We had intended to go back to the boatswain, but we were afraid to take the path through the burning sand once again because of the blazing heat, not counting the fact that we had been treated so badly there. That is why we went to the seashore and sat down on the wet sand.'

53 A soldier — who is unknown, but perhaps the one who was sent on 19 August to Pieter Coene and Barend Bronkhorst to bring them water. On 25 August, no soldier was mentioned, only the creek.
54 Probably *kohl*, still used as a carbon-based protective.

38 – An extremely hot beach and a barrier of cliffs along the Sharqiyah coast south of Ras Al Hadd with some small modern fishing boats and a traditional hut for fishing nets.

Here, at some distance from the coastline, they found an eight-pounder canon. They gathered from this that more ships had run aground here, a conclusion that seemed all the more likely when they found some Dutch cargo knives, a copper grease ladle, a leading block and Moorish rugs in the huts there. Eyks: 'We asked the occupants how they got them. They answered that they had bought them in Muscat.

We then asked them how far it was to Muscat. Some gestured fifteen days, others ten or seven days, and yet others three days. So no estimate could be made.[55] We would do better to stay calm and await a good solution from the Lord. We got some *tamr* and water. On their initiative, our jugs were exchanged for a leather bag. They told us that a Moorish ship from Bengal had once been wrecked there, and that they had seized those articles.'

SATURDAY, 3 SEPTEMBER AND SUNDAY, 4 SEPTEMBER

'We set out again in the morning and had the same encounters as on the last two days.' At this point in the journal, Eyks' entries are very concise; he must have been exhausted, and perhaps this is why he was unable to recount everything in detail. Aside from the frequent body searches, the encounters at this stage of his journey suggest increasing understanding and benevolence on the

---

55 An overhasty conclusion on Eyks' part. The answers are perfectly correct for travel on foot, by camel or by ship. They might have arrived at Al Askharah, a small settlement about 70 km from Hadd, from which it takes another day or two to sail to Muscat.

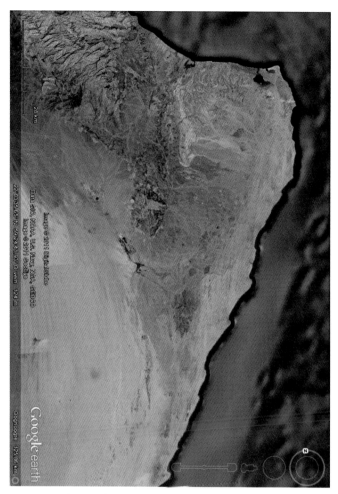

39 – Towards Ras Al Hadd and then, sailing, from Hadd via Sur to Matrah and Muscat. Area c. 140 × 90 km, eye level 125 km.

part of the population, as well as of a certain degree of prosperity. It is a pity that Eyks was unable to recount these meetings in more detail.

MONDAY, 5 SEPTEMBER

The men went further, and came upon huts in which they found only women. They asked them for fire to roast the fish they had been given the day before. They cooked the fish and ate it with relish.

'When the women saw that we were eating the fish with such gusto, they gave us as much *tamr* as we could eat, as well as buttermilk, which they churned in a small leather bag right before our eyes. After this, we went further and came to a large tree (with a low trunk), under which there was a household. We wanted to rest awhile in the shadow of the tree, whereupon the above-mentioned women joined us. They jeered at us and mocked us. We stood up and, although they asked us to stay, we went on our way.' Eyks leaves us to guess at what these women actually meant by their sneers.

At about 3 o'clock in the afternoon, the men came upon four women who were gathering wood. The women wore mules on their feet. 'We asked them for some food and drink, but they motioned to us that we had to go further until we came upon some small huts. We then walked across four paths on which people rode camels every day. Under way we saw various camels loaded with fish that looked like anchovies, but that had been dried. We asked the camel drivers in vain for some fish to eat. We also asked where they came from, whereupon they answered from the village, Eet.'

Eyks did not record whether he had taken Eet as the definitive answer, but it did not take long before he realised that they had reached Hadd.[56] He could not imagine how he would be received there and how he would go further. He still had a long way to go before reaching Muscat, and he must have realised this. In his logbook, Eyks was silent about his presumptions and expectations; he always limited his account to the facts and experiences of the day in question.

He continued in his logbook: 'We kept going until about 7 o'clock. We then saw fires burning, which struck us as unusual. We went there and came upon a hut that had been woven from *tamr* sticks.[57] A man and a woman were sitting in the hut, and a camel lay in front of it. When the people saw us, they gestured that we should come and sit down. They gave us some boiled fish and a drink of water, and showed us the way to some date farmers. We once again followed a light and came upon another such hut, which looked reasonably good and in which two women were sitting. When they saw us they began to scream loudly, whereupon some people came at us, backswords drawn. We stuck out our hands as a sign of friendship. They shook my hand and asked us the same questions as we had been asked in all our previous encounters. When they saw how we were trembling from the cold, they gestured that we should get out of the wind and get behind the hut. There, they gave us *tamr* and water. We asked if we could sleep behind the hut, but they were sympathetic to our plight and brought us to a hut that was open at the top. We slept in it that night.'

---

56 Al Hadd, a village near Ras al Hadd, the low cape at the mouth of the Gulf of Oman. Eyks did not see that cape with its striking fort. He was guided to the natural port of Hadd.
57 Date-palm branches, leaf nerves with the foliage removed.

A cunning merchant captain in Hadd

In the morning, the men saw that they had arrived in a real village: the village of Eet. There were at least a hundred huts, as well as stone warehouses. The men also saw *battils* and *markaps*: Persian-style vessels, according to Eyks. They walked through the whole village, and the people who saw them called out, 'Portugees! Englees! Hollandees!'

'They stopped us and gave us water and *tamr*, and asked us very precise questions. We made it clear to them that we had swum to shore. Eventually, a slave boy came to us, who let us know that we had to go with him. On the way, he told us that another white man had already arrived, a man who walked with a stick. He brought us to a merchant captain. There we found the seaman Jan Theunisze, who had not been able to keep up with the others. He told us that this merchant captain had a vessel on which he was to sail to Musquette or Maskat and from there onwards to Bassora [Basra]. The merchant captain told me the same and asked me if I wanted to go with him to Musquette — or Maskat as it was written on the chart[58] — and he took me to his vessel. He showed me the bags of coffee beans and raw cowhides, as well as his cannons, and asked me if I knew how to fire them. I answered "Yes!" And when he heard that, he told me that if I were willing to go with him, he would engage me as a master gunner and would give me 20 Rupees,[59] and even said that he would employ all of us. Furthermore, he asked me what I had been on the ship. We took some time to understand one another, but after we had had been gesturing for a long time, he understood me and said '*mallem*' [mu'allim], which means *mate* in their language. It suddenly seemed to me as if he did not want to hold us up any longer, because he asked me whether — as soon as I was in Muscat — I would immediately go on to Kharg. I answered him in the affirmative.

That afternoon, he came to me again with his son and said that he would

---

58 Eyks refers here to the chart, used on the AMSTELVEEN. That must have been the nautical map of Van Keulen, but in the copy reproduced at the beginning of this book Muscat was written as Muscatte. Eyks often wrote Maskat or Maskate, but in his time Muscat was also written as Mascate, Maskatte, Muskette, Musquette, Muschette, Muscatte and Musquetta.

59 Rupees, silver Indian coins that were accepted currency along the whole coast (E. Jacobs, 2000, p. 75).

send me to Zoar [Sur] with his son. His son would take me to a captain there, who was going to Masqat and from there to Kharg. After this, he gave his son money for our cargo, and gave us a small basket of *tamr*.

In the afternoon, at about 2 o'clock, we went to the vessel. The captain was not yet ready, however, so we did not depart that day. While our guide (the son of the merchant captain) went back to the village to look for the captain, we stayed in the roadstead under a cliff. Yet neither the captain nor our guide came. Our guide's father sent his slave boy to us with the message that I, with those who could walk that distance, could go back to his warehouse. So the three of us went back and got *tamr* and water from him there. Afterwards, we went to sleep in the warehouse.'

WEDNESDAY, 7 SEPTEMBER

'At sunrise, we again walked with our guide to the vessel. We sailed off to Zoar at 9 o'clock in the morning.' Eyks was sailing again! He must have taken a good look at the surroundings, but he did not make any note in his logbook of what he saw on the way.

THURSDAY, 8 SEPTEMBER

Eyks and his men arrived in Zoar at about 6 o'clock in the evening. They went with their guide to a merchant captain who was soon going to depart for Masqat, and go on from there to Kharg. They stayed on shore that night, where they managed to get hold of some fish, *tamr* and water. Eyks described Sur as a village that was somewhat smaller than the last village, Hadd.

FRIDAY, 9 SEPTEMBER

The men boarded the ship that morning and set sail with six vessels in total. On board, they were given food and drink: *tamr*, a little rice and water.

SATURDAY, 10 SEPTEMBER

In the evening, at sundown, the men arrived in Matrah, a fishing village about one hour west of Muscat. That night, the men slept on board.

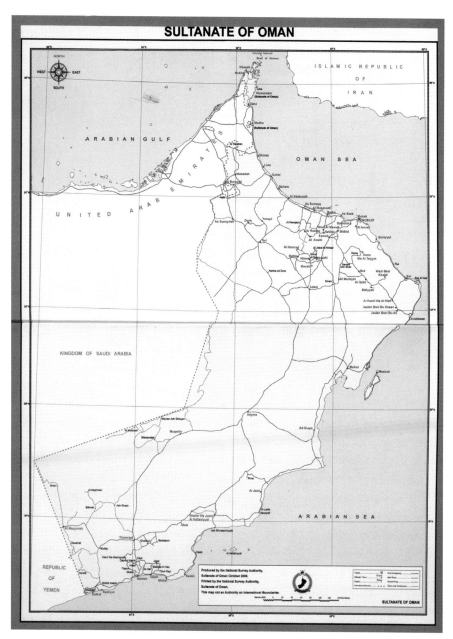

40 – A contemporary road map of Oman. Nowadays, using recently built asphalt roads, the trek of the castaways from Ras Al Madrakah to Ras Al Hadd along the coast of Al Wusta, through the Wahiba dunes and along the Sharqiyah coast can be covered by car. From: Ministry of Information, *Oman 2009-2010*, Muscat 2009.

Arrival in Muscat

SUNDAY, 11 SEPTEMBER

The captain brought the men ashore in the tender, and they set off on foot straight away in their ragged clothing to Muscat. 'Initially we found no one there who could talk to us. The residents shouted after us: *Englis! Portugees! Hollandees! Francees!*[60] As we saw four ships moored in the roadstead, we decided to go there, but on the way we met a black man, who spoke to us in Dutch. He asked us where we came from. I told him that we had lost our ship. He asked if we had been to the agent of the VOC. I replied that I was a stranger here and could not understand the people. He told me that two seamen from our ship had already arrived yesterday.

'He took us to Naraitun, the agent. He asked me where I had lost the ship.[61] After I had given him an account of the accident, he told me to go upstairs. There I found two of my seamen, Matthys Janszen and Jacobus Johannes Balthazar. We were then given food: fish, *tamr*, rice, onions and water. After we had eaten, he gave us some lengths of cloth, so each of us could make a pair of trousers, a shirt and a cap for himself. May the Lord God be praised and thanked for his guidance thus far!'

The agent was very surprised that they had made it so far in a country that, in his view, was populated only by murderers and robbers. He told the men that in the previous year, approximately 35 *Zoar* vessels had run aground, and although each vessel had a crew of 25 to 30 souls, almost all of those people had been murdered. Eyks did not record their reaction to this amazing news. Did they believe Naraitun's tale? If so, they must have wondered why they had been spared.

Because their bodies looked so wretched, Naraitun also gave them bandages for their wounds. He wanted to keep them there for another ten days or so, to allow their bodies to heal, after which he would send them on to Kharg. Eyks agreed with this plan, and immediately wrote a letter to Mr Bosman, the VOC's Trading Post Manager on Kharg, not knowing that he recently had changed his name to Buschman. The letter would be taken there by ship the next day,

60 English! Portuguese! Dutch! French!
61 Please note: this is written *verbatim*. Would the agent have asked him in this way? Might Eyks have been hurt by this? Perhaps he had expected a more honourable greeting.

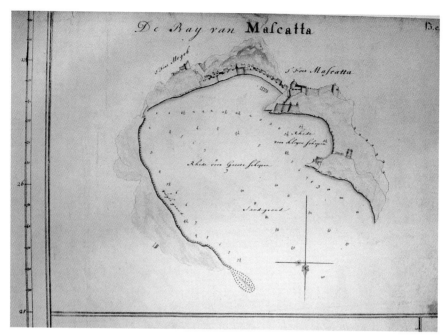

41 – The Bay of Mascatta, an early sketch of the harbour of Muscat on a map in the nautical atlas by Johannes van Keulen, 1763. The original watercolour (1672) is included in the logbook of the *Meerkat*, a small VOC vessel exploring the north coast of Oman in 1666 (B.J. Slot, 1992).

and Eyks also kept a copy of the letter for himself. In the meantime, Eyks heard that two English ships were to arrive there from Basra. He told Naraitun that he would rather leave the next day to avoid other perils.[62] The agent approved of Eyks' plan; after all, their skin would also heal on board. He gave them some food and other provisions for the journey: rice, *tamr*, fish, biscuits, onions, limes, salt and tobacco, as well as a cooking pot and a water jug.

MONDAY, 12 SEPTEMBER

The next morning, Eyks asked the agent if vessels from Muscat would also be going to the wreck. There would be a favourable monsoon on the 20th of the month and an easterly wind would be blowing offshore, meaning that there would be no more breakers. Naraitun answered that he would make a vessel ready for 1,000 Rupiahs.[63] 'Whereupon I asked him if I, one of the others, or everyone together, could go along with them too. To this, however, his reply was: "No!"

On the contrary, we went on board at sundown to depart for Kharg with at least twenty other vessels.'

62 It is not clear to what perils Eyks alluded.
63 He apparently took Eyks' question as a request and turned that into an assignment with a price. Later it would emerge that two ships from Muscat set out for the wreck.

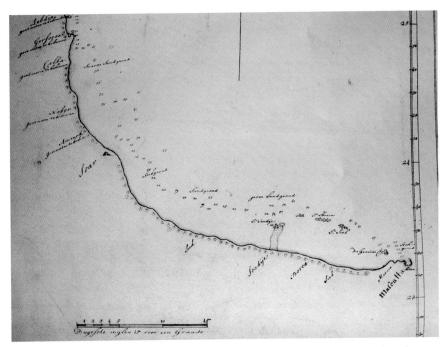

42 – An early Dutch sketch map of the Batinah coast along the Gulf of Oman (1666). From Muscat to Sohar and further northerly with many places (written in portolano style) where 'good water' is available. Depths are given in fathoms (c. 1.80 m). From the Atlas Amsterdam, about 1700 compiled by Isaak de Graaf; facsimile reprint, NA, 2006.

Eyks did not note down anything about the period between 13 and 18 September. He sailed close to the coast, past Sohar and other places, and sailed on further through the Straits of Hormuz to Kharg in the north of the Persian Gulf. On the way, more ships joined their flotilla, which eventually became a merchant fleet of more than 70 ships.

Looking back on these events, it is clear that Eyks was only in Muscat for a very short time. Searching for someone who could understand him, he had walked through the small town, and had seen some ships anchored in the roadstead. He only encountered two natives: a servant (a black man), who spoke to them in Dutch; and the agent, who took care of them, gave them food and provided cloth for clothing. In short, they had returned to civilisation. We can only speculate why Eyks wanted to continue his journey so quickly. While Naraitun was indeed the VOC's agent in Muscat, authority for the Company's affairs was vested in Buschman, the VOC's official representative on Kharg. Eyks may have felt obliged to inform Buschman of the accident as soon as possible.

The awful, seemingly endless trek had unexpectedly come to an end in Hadd. That was a stroke of luck, but Eyks was not confident that all had gone well in Hadd. In his logbook, he noted for the first time that curious villagers

43 – Baghlah's in the roadstead of Muscat c. 1830. Fragment of a sketch by Edmond Paris, *Essai sur la Construction Navale des Peuples Extra-européens*, Paris, 1845. From *Oman, a seafaring nation*, Muscat, 1978.

had asked him for the *exact* place of the accident. The merchant captain, after questioning Eyks, had suddenly changed his plans without giving a reason for doing so. He had swiftly provided a reliable guide for Eyks and the seamen, but he had stayed behind and had not sought any further contact with Eyks. Had he hurried to the wrecked ship after he had understood from Eyks that there had been cannons on board? The monsoon had passed, he knew where to go and, of course, he would have wanted to be the first one there. But was it realistic to think this? The merchant captain had gone to great lengths to get them out of Hadd: he had even given his son money to sail on from Sur to Muscat. After that, however, nothing further had been said to Eyks about the proposal to employ him as a master gunner. It remains guesswork, but would Eyks have suspected something like this and therefore suddenly have been in such a hurry in Muscat?

Moreover, could Naraitun also unwittingly have played a part in this? The agent had immediately rejected Eyks' suggestion that they return together to the wreck, without giving a reason for doing so. Shortly after this incident, though, he quickly agreed to Eyks' proposal to sail on without delay to Kharg. Eyks had told him where the wreck was located and he had said that he would rent a ship that would sail there without delay.

All in all, Eyks spent little time in Muscat. Everywhere along the whole south coast, in Hadd and also in Muscat, he had repeatedly been asked the same question: where had the ship been lost? In his logbook — which he did not start until after his encounter with Buschman — he noted nothing of his thoughts, suspicions or fears. Looking closely, one can nevertheless find clues to support the notion that Eyks had gradually become concerned since Hadd. He was increasingly disturbed by the thought that others might search the wreck to seize anything of value that could still be found; might he be blamed for this?

Unrest in the Arabian merchant fleet

'Today we saw two three-masters, English ships that were bound for Bengal. I asked our captain if I could go on board, and he allowed me to sail to one of the English ships, along with one of the seamen who could speak English. When we got to the ship, the captain asked what business we had on board with him. We shouted to him that we were Dutchmen and had lost our ship. He then said that we could come on board.

Once there, he asked me where we had lost our ship and if we wanted some rice. He then gave us half a bag of rice, six bottles of arak and one full of tea, and six loaves of bread. I requested the captain to be so kind as to inform His Lordship the Director in Bengal, Mr N. Taillefert, orally of our accident, as I did not have any paper on me and the crew of the vessel did not give me any time to write a letter on board. At this, the captain asked me if we wanted to go with him to Bengal, whereupon the cargo would be given to us as a gift. We thanked him nonetheless for his kindness, because we were already so close to the Company's trading post for which our ship was bound; we therefore went back to our vessel.'

FRIDAY, 23 SEPTEMBER

They dropped anchor between Cabo Bardestant and Congo in the Bay of Deyr, a bay to the south-east of Kharg. The merchant fleet now consisted of two *guraps*[64] and about 75 *battils*: Zoar vessels and *markabs*.

After they had been waiting there for six days, Eyks asked the captain why he did not sail on to Kharg. According to the captain, Dutch and Persian merchants[65] were conspiring to steal the Zoar vessels. 'Upon hearing this, I shook my head. No way, and if things went that far, we would help them fight. We consulted actively on board every day. They wanted to transfer me and my men to the two- and three-mast *guraps* as master gunners, and would pay us Rupiahs for this on arrival in Basra. We did not know whom they were at war with, however. It could also be our own nation, because they locked their forefingers together like hooks and said: "*Kareek en Boesher zam zamma poe poe grap!*"

64 Guraps [khoorab] are Arabian freighters with two or three masts, without a lion and pointed in front, and 75 smaller vessels (*battil*'s and *markab*'s) from Sur and Muscat.
65 Eyks wrote *Baljoosje* and *Miermannie*. This means: Dutch and Persian merchants.

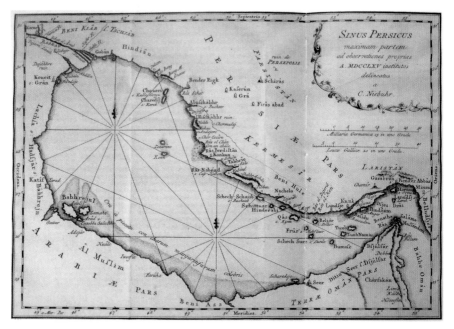

44 – The Persian Gulf with Basra in the north and Kharg (Charedsj, say Karek) close to the Persian coast and from there, west to east, Abuschehhr (Bushir), Ras Berdistan (Cabo Bardestant), Konkun (Congo), the Bay of Dahhr (Deyr), Gamron, Bender Abbas (Bandar Abbasi) and Ormuz (Hormus). This map was designed just after the period Eyks sailed here twice: In 1763 on an Arabian merchants' fleet to Kharg and back on the snow *De Courier* to Cochin at the Malabar Coast. He returned in 1764 on the East Indiamen Lekkerkerk, again in the service of the VOC. Map by Carsten Niebuhr, *Beschreibung von Arabien*, 1772. Niebuhr visited Kharg in 1765.

which means that Kharg and Bushir [Dutch and Persian merchants] were conspiring and going to shoot at the guraps. We made it clear that we did not agree with them, but that was nevertheless a reason for them to want to return to Muscat.' Yet the captains did not do so immediately.

The original text is not clear in all respects, something that is also evident from the passage above. Eyks did let us know that he was troubled by his inability to understand the Arabs.

THURSDAY, 29 SEPTEMBER

'We saw three vessels coming towards us. The captains thought they were *Miermanie gallowets* (Persian galleys). All of the ships readied themselves for battle. The galleys fired three salute shots from a distance as a sign of friendship, but this was not understood. The 75 vessels set sail and formed a crescent to surround the three. Thereupon one of the three, a *bagaar*, sailed on to the middle of the crescent to the *guraps* with a letter from Kharg, and hailed various Zoar vessels. They shouted to them that the other two ships were two *gallowets* of *baljoostje*, which means that they were *galleys of merchants*, for they call a merchant a *baljoost*.'

Here, Eyks displays his familiarity with types of Arabian, Persian and Indian ships, but he does not go into their specific characteristics. Nowadays a traditional Arabian cargo ship tends to be called a dhow, *but experts distinguish between many different kinds. A* baqarah *or* baggarah *does not have a deep draught, and was chiefly used in the Gulf for fishing and coastal trade. A* gurap [gharab] *is larger; with this, Eyks seems to be referring to a deep-draught* baghlah *or* ghanjah. *Just like the somewhat smaller* sambuq, *these ships were also used for ocean crossings to African and around India. Acquaintance with various types of Portuguese ships and, much later, the establishment of the British East India Company's shipyard in Bombay, strongly influenced shipbuilding in the Gulf region. In Oman, larger ships were mainly built in Sur.*

Oman, a seafaring nation (1979).

Eyks understood the exchange: the ships had come to convoy them, because the Company sold them many goods each year. They had feared that the vessels would not go to Kharg because the sailors had been deceived into thinking that *baljoost* (Dutch merchants) were conspiring with the *Miermanie,* which was not true. 'When the galleys came towards us, I saw that they were waving Prince flags,[66] and I said to the captain: they're Dutch! We stood together and when the galley *Verfvisch* passed us, we were asked where we came from. I shouted: "from the wrecked ship *Amstelveen!*" The message was passed on to the galley *Revengie,* on which Joseph Ramma was the master. He commanded his yawl to be rowed to me forthwith, so that I could board his ship. He received me in a friendly manner and sent the yawl immediately back to pick up the others. They were taken onto the other galley. Then the whole fleet set sail.'

That was how things happened those days. Naraitun had arranged and paid for their passage, but the whole fleet had narrowly escaped returning to Muscat without having achieved its aim, due to a combination of unfounded rumours, fear, misunderstandings (the Arabs did not use flags) and faulty communication.

Eyks and his men were taken to Kharg on the small Company vessels. They had achieved their aim in a dignified manner, and this must have been a source of pleasure for them, especially Eyks. Their courageous, and at times horrendous, survival trek from Mataraca to the civilised world — to Muscat and Kharg —

66 Prince flag — the Dutch tricolour.

45 – An endless beach north in the Gulf of Masirah...

had ended, but was to have a long and nasty aftermath.

Fortunately, they travelled on quickly. After all, at that time, one never knew quite what might happen in a foreign country. In fact, hardly anyone knew that they had wandered around for many weeks. Eyks and his men might not even have realised that they were probably the first Europeans to cross this part of the Arabian Desert. Walking barefoot, no less, in unbearable heat, across sharp, hot rocks, high cliffs and endless barren, shadeless beaches, enduring days on end without food and drink, having to leave comrades behind who were unable to go on, usually with empty, wooden jugs on their burnt shoulders, constantly troubled by small groups of harsh Bedouin who threatened them with weapons. Only after about three weeks of such suffering did they occasionally enjoy a warm welcome and generous help from poor, kindly fishermen's families along the northern part of the coastal strip. For most of the men, the agony ended in Hadd.

Never before had anyone completed that journey with neither a map nor a compass, nor food nor drink for days on end, unable to understand or speak a word of the local language, lacking camels, weapons and fishing gear; without anything to exchange and, after a week or two, even almost without clothing, lacking anything to put on their heads as protection against the heat of the sun. In Muscat, hardly anyone was aware of the men's unique feat, and they all travelled on as quickly as possible. In this, Naraitun played his part; well over a year later, he met a seaman from the *Amstelveen*, who had finally arrived in Muscat, and took him in disguise as quickly as possible on board a VOC ship that was anchored there in the roadstead. By coincidence, this was precisely the same ship on which Eyks had sailed back from Batavia to Muscat.

Eyks must have been aware of the uniqueness of their experience during the survival trek. Indeed, we owe his logbook to this realisation, and in particular to the idea that others might learn something from it, should they ever end up in such circumstances. As a result, we have been given an opportunity to give this phenomenal achievement its well-earned place in the maritime history of Oman, as well as in the canon of the national history of the Netherlands.

With the Resident on Kharg

MONDAY, 3 OCTOBER

At sundown, they anchored in the roadstead of Kharg. Eyks wrote only one short sentence about what happened that evening: 'I then went ashore to the Trading Post Manager there, Mr Buschman, to whom I gave an account of my journey.'

What happened during that crucial evening? Eyks does not even let us know Buschman's response. Eyks continues wryly: 'The snow *De Courier*, Captain *Lasboom*, also arrived here in the roadstead from Bassora. The Lord God be praised for our arrival, thus far!'

TUESDAY, 4 OCTOBER

The next day, only 'six men were re-employed and registered as:

ƒ14   *Carsten Pietersze*, from *Heir*, Gun servant,[67] 1763
ƒ14   *Willem Nicolson*, from *'s Hertogenbosch*, Gun servant, 1763
ƒ9   *Matthys Janszen*, from *Dantzig*, Seaman, 1763
ƒ9   *Jan Theunisze*, from *Luxemburg*, Seaman, 1763
ƒ11   *Jansz. Andreas Kolstrop*, from *Dronthem*, Gun servant on OUD-CARSPEL, according to Ord: 1762
ƒ7   *Jacobus Johannes Balthazar*, from *Wetteren*, apprentice on the HUIS DE BOEDE, according to Ordinance Anno 1762.'

Eyks then noted in his logbook: 'The Trading Post Manager, Mr Buschman, told me it would be better for me and the boatswain's mate, Pieter van Holland, to go on the freeburgher's snow *De Courier* to Malabar[68] or Ceylon, because there was no employment for us there, and we would have to rely on expenses from the Company. I then told Mr Buschman that I would obey him as he saw fit. So I left without a job.'

---

67 Gun servant (*bosschieter*) — experienced seaman who can also operate a *bus* (ship's cannon).
68 Malabar — southwest coast of India; freeburgher's snow — small freighter belonging to someone who had settled in the charter area of the VOC as a free citizen after his contract had expired.

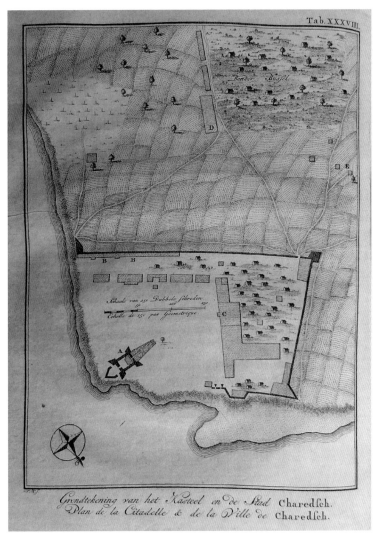

Tab. XXXVIII.

46 – Fort Mosselstein on Kharg in 1765. Engraving after a drawing by C. Niebuhr, Part 2 (1780). The Persian name Kharg was written as Charedsch.

Eyks must have been rather disappointed by his reception at Fort Mosselstein, to put it mildly. What was discussed on the first evening can be derived, to a certain extent, from the letter that Buschman wrote to Batavia the following day. That letter contained little more information than Eyks had already written to Buschman. Had Eyks intentionally only told him some of the main issues? Or did Buschman, concerned about the profit that was evading him, hold back from continuing to ask questions about the accident and the journey along the coast? He may have refrained from doing so because Eyks' employment and pay had been discontinued from the day that the ship ran aground — such were the rules. It was none of his business. If anything happened that evening, and if so, what, then this cannot be gathered from Eyks' logbook. The

Snaauwschip Zeijlende voer de wind

47 – A snow sailing with the wind. Eyks wrote his *Notes* as a passenger on the snow *De Courier*, sailing via Gamron and Muscat to Cochin, thus on a rather small ship like this. His voyage is indicated in the VOC area map on p. 18. From: G. Groenewegen, 1789.

fact that after having experienced so many horrors, suffering and deprivation, Eyks disposed of the meeting with a short, insignificant sentence may indicate that the short confrontation with the VOC's official representative had been an unexpected blow. Instead of receiving a token of appreciation for reporting the accident so quickly, Eyks was told that he would go to Batavia jobless and without pay; not as a paid naval officer in appropriate dress, but without any status and in self-made clothing, on a much smaller vessel that did not even belong to the Company.

Did the two men perhaps not get along? Was Buschman furious because the whole cargo had been lost? Did Buschman consider Eyks to be the man responsible for this loss? Or did Buschman blame him in some way for already having told Naraitun the position of the wreck? At any rate, an expedition to salvage the cannons and the anchors of the *Amstelveen* was no longer considered worthwhile.

After a 15–day stay on Kharg, Eyks took leave of Mr Buschman at sunrise on Wednesday, 19 October. He did not note down anything in his logbook about his stay in Fort Mosselstein and his farewell to Kharg. He went on board *De Courier* with Captain N. Lasboom, and sailed that very day to Bandar Abbasi, also known as Gamron.

Salt from Bandar Abbasi

De Courier anchored in the roadstead of Bandar Abbasi on Friday, 28 October, to load salt. There had been a Company trading post in Gamron on the Strait of Ormuz for years. In 1753, however, the VOC relocated its trading activities to Kharg. Eyks found a Company *logie* there, managed by a European.

GAMRON oder   BENDER ABASSI.

1. *Die Holländische Wohnung.* 2. *die Englische.* 3. *die Französische.* 4. *Mestzid oder Moschèe.* 5 *Das Castell.* 6. *das Fort.* 7. *Der berg Ginau*

48 – Gamron or Bandar Abbasi, the strategically situated Persian harbour on the Straits of Hormuz. One out of 14 pictures around a German chart of Persia, in 1762 engraved by J.B. Homann after an unknown, probably much earlier source. In the midst the abandoned VOC quarters (called 'logie'), a large warehouse that sometimes functioned as temporary accommodation. The estates of deceased seamen were also auctioned there. The warehouse dated from the time that Gamron was an important port in the Gulf for VOC ships. After the VOC started to use Fort Mosselstein on Kharg, the influence of the English in Gamron increased. They attacked the warehouse and partially destroyed it. The custodian, Jan Jacob Christant, suffered substantial losses which Buschman, at Batavia's insistence, had to try and recover from the British (missive dd. 24 May 1764, inv. no. 1018). Next to this large building the much smaller offices of the British and French East India Companies. Eyks ascended the mountain Ginau in November 1763.

Eyks' mood had softened by this point, and he felt like a free man. Free from the constraints of employment, he could go wherever he pleased. In the meantime — maybe already on Kharg — he had started his *Notes*: a logbook in which he recorded the disaster, their trek along the desert coast and the aftermath. In any case, he now had paper and writing materials at his disposal, and on board he had plenty of time to write. He even took the time to go on a special outing, perhaps with Pieter van Holland, because he uses the first-person plural in his account: 'We found a mountain here two hours inland on which we saw four rarities, namely salt, which flowed from the top of the mountain like glass, but also Indian red, sulphur and black, gleaming sand. All this on one mountain! Close to the mountain, we found a well with water that was so hot that one could hardly put one's hands in it, and we discovered that Indians[69] still brought offerings here.'

A few days later, the calm on *De Courier* was shattered. 'We stayed in the roadstead until Thursday, 2 December. On that day, nine galleys from the island of Ormuz came towards us to attack us, because we did not want to load any of their salt, but instead had hired people ourselves to get salt. Hereupon we made everything ready for battle, but because the wind was not favourable for us we fully braced ourselves and sailed away from there at night.' Eyks did not mention their destination.

69 Here: inhabitants of the Indian subcontinent.

A surprising reunion in Muscat

On Saturday, 4 December, *De Courier* departed for Muscat. The snow arrived there a week later, and anchored in the roadstead. Naraitun came on board. On this occasion, Eyks asked him whether the vessel he had sent to the location of the wreck had already returned. 'He answered me that of the two vessels he had sent there, one had come back with goods: 19 beams and boards, 106 tin ingots, 13 baskets of spices of different kinds and some other goods. I asked him if he would be so kind as to let me note all this down. He said he would do so when I came ashore. After being on shore twice and asking him three times to let me note down the goods, however, I got no answer from him, and went back on board having failed to achieve my aim. I then heard from him that another seaman from the wrecked ship was ashore: he had gone blind. He also told me that at the place where our ship had run aground, the Arabs had fought and killed each other over the goods, and that 400 of them had lost their lives. And that all of the drowned Europeans had washed up on the beach, and they had also seen other goods lying on the ground.'

What exactly had happened on the beach? Where were the cannons, and why had nothing been said about them? And why had the anchors, which were apparently still lying there, not been taken along? The story about the Arabs having fought each other over the goods, and 400 deaths, appears rather far-fetched against the background of Eyks' experiences with the Bedouin during their walk. What had become of the second vessel, and why had Eyks heard nothing about other vessels at the site?[70]

The identity of the seaman who had gone blind could not be established. Apparently nobody, including Eyks, looked after him because he had become incapacitated for work. Although another seaman had better luck...

On Monday, 13 December, the seaman Steven Hillekens from Deventer came on board. This was an exceptional coincidence; to have stumbled across the ship that was carrying Eyks and the boatswain's mate, which did not even belong to the VOC. It was an excellent opportunity to learn more about his fate and that of the others. Eyks noted down Hillekens' story in detail.

---

70 According to Slot (1993), this was a galley belonging to Sheikh Khalfan. A galley (with oarsmen) is usually faster than a *sailing vessel*. All the same, the galley had not yet returned, which also raises a number of questions.

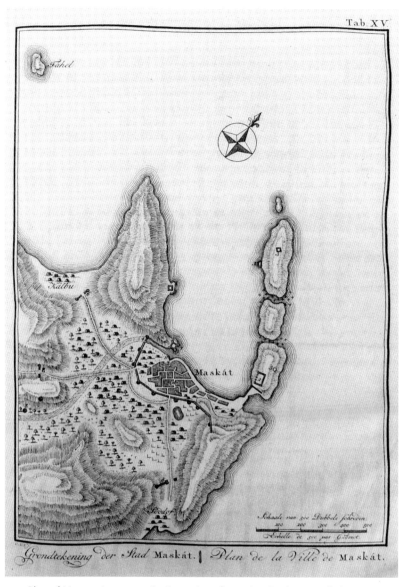

Tab. XV.

49 – Plan of Muscat, January 1765. Engraving after a drawing by C. Niebuhr, II, 1780.

'He was one of those whom we had lost on 17 August. He told us that he had made his journey to Muscat entirely on foot in two days less than three months. He, too, had stumbled along in misery, sometimes without having eaten or drunk for seven days, and his body was also burnt from head to toe. He had also been in the mountains that we passed on 22 August, and had found Jan Drevens lying dead between the rocks. And young Bronkhorst lay near him, practically dead from hunger and thirst. He was still conscious, however, and told him that the said seaman (Jan Drevens) had died the day before; and that he would like to go with him, but could not do so because of thirst. He

(Steven Hillekens) also told us that the surgeon's second mate, Pieter Coene, had passed away.'

Eyks summarised his findings that day as follows: Steven Hillekens was the twenty-second man to have made it along the coast. One man had eventually died in Muscat and the others had joined various English and Dutch ships and vessels. We do not know how and when Eyks found this out. He must have included information in his logbook that he later received in Batavia and, even later, when he was back in Muscat.

Steven Hillekens sailed together with Eyks on *De Courier* to Cochin, and from there on to Batavia.

On his way to Kharg, in September, Eyks had staid only two days in Muscat. When he arrived, tired and hungry, he did not have much of an eye for where he was and what he saw, and this was also the case when he left Muscat with the Arabian fleet. He had sewn new clothes, written a letter and spent one night there. Now, nearly three months later, rested and relaxed, he took a fresh look at the seaport; mainly from the roadstead, as befits a seaman, but he also went ashore a few times, for example with Naraitun. He kept his eyes open. On board, he also took a good look at the landscape around him. Perhaps he had also read something about the country (possibly in Fort Mosselstein), or heard more about it here on shore. This can be gathered from what he wrote in his logbook. Eyks was a sailor in heart and soul, but he also knew how to write. The following passage is one of the most elegant in the *Notes*.

50 – Muscat in 1811. Watercolour, unknown artist. Taken from D. Howarth, 1977.

'While here, I saw that Muscat lies between the mountains. Four castles with watch houses had been built on them. It has a fine port, a bay. We Dutchmen usually call Muscat "Musquette." It is a reasonably large and well-known trading town on the Gulf of Ormuz on the Arabian coast, and is inhabited by Arabs, Indians and Jews. Muscat is considered the most powerful country of the Arabian principalities. It is located to the east of *Arabia Felix*, so called because of its fertility compared to *Arabia Petraea* and *Arabia Deserta*. Because we kept to our path along the coast, however, we had to trek through the most desolate and sandy regions. Nevertheless, by the grace of God, we found a shortcut. This is evident from the fact that, another year later, it was discovered that some of my companions had even roamed around for more than a year in the middle of the lands of the savage, greedy Arabs, who lead only a nomadic life and recognise their tribal chiefs and leaders as their only sovereigns. They, too, were saved, nonetheless.'

At this point in the logbook, Eyks again calmly summarised what had happened to him and his men, and described the features of the places in which it occurred, who lived there and what life was like beyond the prosperous north coast. It is not possible to deduce from his *Notes* which of the shipwrecked seamen eventually reached Muscat, who died on the way to Hadd, or who was held against their will (such as the little Javanese boy, for example). But the fact that, every now and then, yet another person from the ship arrived in Muscat, must have done him good and been a source of relief to him. After all, they too had been saved by the grace of God.[71]

---

71 Eyks wrote that he would deal with *their* experience further on in the logbook; but he mentioned only one (on 26 August 1765).

To Batavia by way of Cochin

On Saturday, 18 December, *De Courier* sailed from Muscat to Cochin on the southwest coast of India. The boat arrived there on Sunday, 22 January 1764. In the roadstead were moored two large VOC ships: the *Erf-Prins* and the *Vreedestein*.

Two days later, Commander Weyerman summoned Eyks to tell him what had happened. At his request, Eyks gave him an extract from the logbook regarding the wreckage of the *Amstelveen*. Commander Weyerman decided that Eyks should go on one of the ships to Batavia, and immediately made arrangements for this. This decision also applied to the other two crewmen,

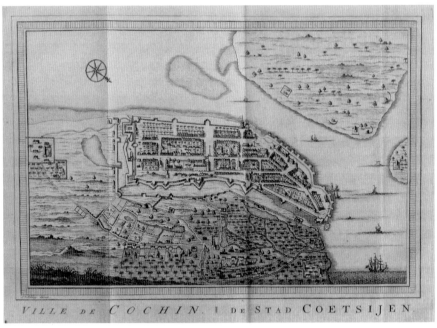

VILLE DE COCHIN. DE STAD COETSIJEN.

51 – Cochin on the Malabar Coast, a walled VOC settlement on the west coast of India that had been captured from the Portuguese. Ships lay in the roadstead at the height of the compass rose that is sketched on the map. For many centuries the town of Cochin, which was situated further inland along the river, was visited by ships from Oman and Persia to buy wood and rope, or to have repairs carried out. Engraving from *Historische Beschryving der Reizen* [Historical description of travel], published by Wed. S Schouten en Zoon, J. Hayman, J. Roman et al., Part 16, 1757.

the boatswain's mate and the seaman. An Ordinance dated 27 January 1764 decreed that they were placed on the *Erf-Prins* to be 'transported to Batavia, and to do duty to earn their livelihood.'

It is evident from a memorandum in the VOC archives that this decision was felt to be a punishment; at any rate, this was the interpretation given by a subordinate Company servant in Batavia, who recorded the decision thus in the pay book. Eyks and the other two men probably also perceived the decision as a punishment, albeit, of course, an undeserved one. They had to do duty without any work agreement and did not receive any pay, even though they were not to blame for what had occurred; on the contrary.

A day later, the three men boarded the *Erf-Prins*, which was commanded by Captain Pieter Schooneman. The heavily-armed freighter was to sail direct from Cochin to Batavia with 64 European seamen, 23 Moorish seamen, 27 European soldiers and eight passengers on board; a total of 122 souls.

Three weeks later, the *Erf-Prins* was still in the roadstead. Flag signals had indicated that pirates had been sighted who threatened to attack them from the north. The crew received instructions from the shore and made many preparations, in case they should have to fight. The next morning, on Thursday, 23 February, the captain came on board. The sails were set upon yarns — fastened in such a way that they could be raised quickly — so the ship could put out to sea immediately if the pirates should arrive. Everything that could serve as defence was made ready. Flag signals were sent back and forth with instructions, orders, requests and the latest news about the pirates, who were said to be eight *guraps* and 30 galleys strong. In short, the crew expected an attack. The attack ultimately failed to occur, because the monsoon had passed before the pirates. The *Erf-Prins* had even diverted its course to the south for safety's sake, but after well over a week, when the danger had passed, she returned from the roadstead of Coulang to Cochin. Meanwhile, it was already nearly mid-March when the ship was made ready for departure. She raised anchor on 31 March to sail to Batavia.

A few days later, on 6 April 1764, the boatswain's mate, Pieter van Holland from Rotterdam, died. Eyks simply stated this in his logbook. He avoided sentiment, as he almost always did. But no doubt Eyks must have thought back on the perilous situation just before the bow of the *Amstelveen* had been smashed to pieces. After all, it had been Pieter van Holland who had saved him from certain death by cutting his heavy, soaking tailcoat off his body.

On Tuesday, 22 May, at 3 o'clock in the afternoon, the *Erf-Prins* with Eyks and Steven Hillekens on board anchored in the roadstead of Batavia. Eyks had gone over seven months without pay and wrote, evidently thankful and relieved, in his logbook: 'Praise and thank the Lord for a safe voyage, thus far!'

52 – Negapatnam on the east coast of India (Coromandel), one of the most important settlements in the western trade area of the VOC. Engraving, W. Schouten, 1676.

53 – The roadstead of Batavia and *Het Casteel* (The Castle) where Eyks and Daalberg were
questionned. Shortly after both men were reappointed in the service of the VOC. Engraving
(c. 1690) taken from F. Valentijn, *Oud en Nieuw Oost-Indiën*, IV, A, p. 228.

Eyks did not record a word about his stay in Batavia in his logbook. He was even silent about Jonas Daalberg, the boatswain who had sailed directly from Muscat to Batavia. Together, the two men were examined by a committee of inquiry. Their statements were compared with a concise account of the interrogation of two seamen, Hendrik Poolman and Jan Brinkhout, who had sailed from Muscat to Bengal on an English freighter. On the whole, the two statements agreed with one other. The interrogators' conclusion was summarised in a Resolution of 15 June 1764. The opinion was that the authorities on board (that is, the captain and the first mate, even though this was not stated explicitly) had been 'negligent.' They had not used the sounding lead when they had been in sight of the coast, nor had they attempted to sail away from the coast or to anchor when the fog set in again. It was then decided to allow the pay of the saved crew members, including the five seamen who remained in Batavia, to be started again as soon as they were re-employed.

For the VOC, this inquiry closed the matter of the *Amstelveen*. The record of the interrogation of the two seamen in Coromandel, as summarised by the Governor of Coromandel in Nagapatnam, functioned as a guideline for the Resolution. The questioning of Eyks and Daalberg seems to have contributed little, a fact that is remarkable in itself. Did the captains on the committee of inquiry say absolutely nothing about the ship's remarkable deviation from the prescribed sailing route to the Gulf? Did they not go on to ask about the reasons for not sounding, and did Eyks not say anything about this?[72] Did the captains fail to ask him about the role played by the first mate during that fatal evening watch, when the ship went adrift in calm conditions and ran aground? The conciseness of the Resolution gives the impression that the High Government of the VOC was no longer really interested in what had actually happened, or that it might even have had something to hide. Given the number of victims, it was relatively easy to dismiss the matter as an unfortunate accident for which those responsible could no longer be held liable.

Eyks and Daalberg were apparently satisfied with this outcome. Both men were re-employed quickly. At that time, Batavia was faced with a serious shortage of crew on its ships.

72 An honest answer would have implied serious criticism of the Company, particularly the equipage master in Batavia, who happened to be a member of the committee of inquiry. He was especially to blame for the ship's poor state of repair. Did this concurrence cause Eyks' absolute silence during the interrogation in Batavia?

To Muscat once again

On 18 June 1764, again with the rank of third mate, Eyks was engaged on the ship *Lekkerland*, under the command of Captain Christiaan Blom. Once again, he was on a ship that was bound for Kharg. They departed on Saturday, 30 June at half-past-six in the morning; the *Lekkerland* saluted the roadstead with eleven cannon shots and was thanked by the Admiral Ship with three shots in return. A week later, on the afternoon of 7 July, she was on the high seas and commencing her voyage across the Indian Ocean.

Seven weeks later, on 25 August, the easternmost castle[73] of Muscat was sighted. The captain decided to put in at the Bay of Muscat, because many of the crew were ill and ten crew members had already died during the voyage. In addition, they needed fresh fruit and water. The wind and current forced them to anchor almost 2 km from the coast; there, the dinghy and the longboat were put out. A marvellous event occurred a day later...

'On Sunday, 26 August 1764, we had the junior seaman, Barend Bronkhorst, on board. He was one of my former crew on the ship that was lost on 5 August 1763, the *Amstelveen*. On 11 December 1763, I had recorded that he had been found by Steven Hillekens, lying almost dead, near the lifeless body of Jan Drevens. Barend Bronkhorst told me that the Arabs had picked him up and carried him along, and cared for him with food and drink, and that was how he had managed to stay alive. He had arrived in Muscat only seven days ago.'

Barend Bronkhorst gave Eyks a detailed account of what he had gone through. 'He had been forced to work for the Arabs for a few months in their household. They had also circumcised him against his will. He finally managed to escape by hiding under a fishing net in a vessel that was ready to depart, without knowing where it would go. He concealed himself for four to six days without eating much, and meanwhile heard that they were sailing to Muscat. They arrived safely there, and after the captain and the others had gone on shore, he saw a chance to escape from the ship. He went to the agent of the VOC, Mr Naraitun, who gave him food and drink and dressed him in Turk-ish-style clothes. Immediately after the ship arrived, he [Naraitun] took him

---

73 Fort Jalali. Eyks called it a castle, probably because it was built high above sealevel. For men at sea it was an important point of reference. During the VOC-era a fort in Asia was a walled trading post meant for accommodation for employees and storage of commodities.

on board, disguised as a Turk.' One can only speculate at the reasons for such secrecy; perhaps helping a slave to escape was a punishable offence, but Eyks says nothing about this.

It had taken Barend Bronkhorst well over a year to do so, but he had made it to Muscat! He was put on a Dutch ship that had happened to arrive at almost the same time, and which happened to have Eyks on board. While recalling memories of their gruelling walk along the south coast, did the two men ever wonder whether more seamen had perhaps managed to reach Muscat without being noticed? In his logbook, however, Eyks limited himself to the facts. That day, he concluded the account of the seaman's story that day in his typical way: 'We stayed there in the roadstead and took in water.'

On Friday, 31 August, they weighed anchor just before evening, and sailed to Kharg. 'We saw that an English ship which had come from Bombay and wanted to go to Basra also left the roadstead and followed us.'

The *Lekkerkerk* arrived in the roadstead of Kharg on 11 October 1764, and was immediately made ready to unload the cargo. Two days later, the domestic fleet arrived from Mecca, and on Sunday, 14 October, a fleet of fourteen ships arrived, which departed the next day for Basra. Kharg could occasionally be quite a busy free port. The cargo of the *Lekkerkerk* was unloaded, and a new cargo and fresh supplies were taken on board. On Monday, 3 November, Cap-

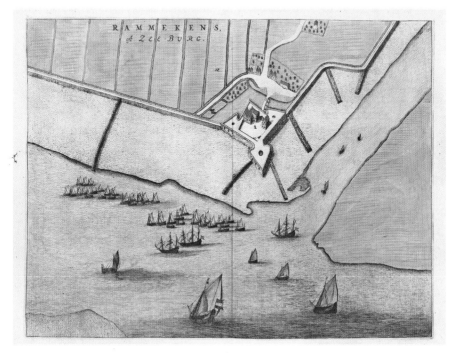

54 – The roadstead of Rammekens *('Vlakke van Rammekens')* with three East Indiamen anchored near the entrance of the canal to Middelburg and several smaller vessels sailing or waiting.

tain Blom and Resident Buschman came on board, together with some other acquaintances of Eyks' from Kharg.[74] In the afternoon, the anchor was weighed and the ship set sail to return to Batavia. She arrived there safe and sound on 2 April 1765.

Afterwards, Eyks made another short trip on the same ship to Cheribon on Java. He returned to Zeeland on the ship *Zuid-Beveland*, under the command of Captain Huibregt van der Kneu, by way of the Cape of Good Hope. He arrived there on 16 May 1766, at Rammekens, the roadstead of Vlissingen near Middelburg. 'We praise and thank the Lord for keeping us and guiding us to this safe port of our desire!'

With this, Eyks ended his logbook.

74 The Manager (Buschman) and other acquaintances... here Eyks wrote something for the first time about Kharg, the ship's movements there and the people he had got to know.

Back in Middelburg at last

Cornelis Eyks was home again, in Middelburg, on the familiar Kraanstraat. His fourth voyage to the East had come to an end. This time, however, he had something to tell: a true story. How might he go about it? What he said would have to be true. Perhaps, if his story were to be doubted, he would be better off not saying anything. Keeping silent might be wiser in that case.

Eyks' homecoming was thus different from previous times, and he himself also seemed to have changed a great deal. His skin was different and he was quieter than he had been. He had often wondered on board the *De Courier* and the *Lekkerland,* but mainly on his voyage home on the *Zuid-Beveland,*[75] how and to whom he would recount the events of three years previously on the south coast of Arabia, his experiences in the high breakers, on the windy beach and then for weeks in the desert? Anyone who had not been there would be almost incapable of understanding it. Could he actually tell everyone everything? Did he have to? All of those deaths, and those men who had been left behind on the way; it had been horrible, but they had had no choice.

What was already known in Middelburg about the shipwreck of the *Amstelveen*? As far as Eyks could remember, there had only been two men from Walcheren (Zeeland) on board, both from Middelburg: he himself and Pieter Coene, the surgeon's second mate. Pieter Coene had died near Hadd. The news of his death must have reached Middelburg by way of the pay office; a settlement usually had to be made after a death, so the sad news was spread in that way. No one, however, knew that the bay man had not drowned when the ship went aground. On the contrary, he had survived the trial on the bowsprit and had gone courageously on his way with the others. After about four weeks, however, Coene had fallen seriously ill and had walked back, completely exhausted, to the Arab family on the beach who had shown them so much kindness and generosity. He had made this decision in the hope that he could recover, following the advice that Eyks had given him the evening before. Only much later did Eyks hear that Pieter Coene had died there, left behind with benevolent people whom he could not understand. The advice was surely meant well, but after taking his leave, he had gone on with the others. How could he tell this

75 A homeward-bounder of the Chamber of Zeeland.

55 – Middelburg on Walcheren seen from the south. Right the city harbour with some ships. Engraving after a design by C. Pronk, Tirion, 1760.

sad story to the bay man's family, his relatives at home and his fellow townsmen, again and again?

Some time previously, when he realised that he could write well, Eyks had already decided to publish his *Notes* as a short book. Not for his own glory, of course, nor as a tall tale of the high seas, but very modestly as a lesson for all who might at some time end up in similar dangerous and distressing circum-

56 – Middelburg, city view with the Oostkerk *(East Church)* in the second half of the 18th century, Augsburg, G.B. Probst, 1770.

NOODLOTTIGE GEVALLEN

Aan het gefalveerde Volk van het Ed:
Oost-Indisch Compagnies Schip

AMSTELVEEN,

Na deszelfs Verongelukken in dato 5. Augustus
1763., op de Tocht van Batavia *na* Perfiën,
op hun weg door Arabiën *overgekomen;*

Alles volgens de beknopte en echte
Aantekeningen van

CORNELIS EYKS,

Toen Derdewaak *op gemelden Bodem.*

De Koninglyke Propheet in Pf. CVII: 23—30.
van *die met Schepen ter Zee afvaren, han-*
del dryvende op groote Wateren, fprekende, be-
fluit zyn verhaal der benauwdheden, welke dezelve gemeenelyk moeten ondergaan, met in het **31.**
en **32.** vers hunne plicht hen bekend te maken, door
te zeggen: *Laat ze voor den HEERE zyne goe-*
dertierenheid loven, ende zyne wonderwerken voor
de Kinderen der Menfchen. Ende hem verhoogen,
in de Gemeinte des Volks, ende in het geftoelte der
Oudften hem roemen. Om my van deze algemee-
ne verplichting te kwyten, had ik wel voorgenomen
de volgende byzondere Gevallen, welke my en het
ontkomen Volk zyn overgekomen, ter verheerly-
king van 's Heeren goedheid over my, aan de We-
reld als een Stukje op zig zelfs gedrukt mede te
deelen; dog ziende dat het zelve daartoe van een
te klein beflag was, heb ik die *Aantekening*, op

B b   den

57 – Frontpage of the *Notes* of Cornelis Eyks, in Tydkorting, 1766, p. 365-418.

stances.[76] Seamen had known for many years that when a ship returned from a long voyage, a publisher might be standing on the quay, looking for someone who could describe an exciting adventure, preferably a true story that would entertain the reader and make some money. Such publishers were sometimes even willing to write the stories down for their narrators in proper Dutch.[77]

No one knew what Eyks had gone through, nor about the logbook that he had kept. Even in Holland, almost nothing was known about the shipwreck of the *Amstelveen* and the survivors' experiences. After coming home, Eyks soon became aware that telling the complex story in the right way would be a hopeless task. He was not accustomed to speaking for a long time, and therefore quickly decided to offer his *Notes* to the only publisher he knew, Jeroen van der Sande, who had a well-established bookshop on the Grote Markt in Middelburg. While Van der Sande thought the text too short for a book, the *Notes* were perfectly suited to publication as one of his monthly instalments for subscribers,[78] and also, afterwards, for inclusion in an anthology of these stories. Eyks' logbook was thus published at the end of 1766, and probably distributed mainly on Walcheren and the other Zeeland islands. In that rather small circle, however, the book soon passed into oblivion and the story became forgotten.

The anthology with Eyks' *Notes* also included an account of a voyage undertaken by a Swedish botanist to the Middle East and the Holy Land. Just like his famous fellow countryman Linnaeus, he was very interested in the medicinal herbs growing there, and went to look for their seeds. An apothecary in Ostend (Belgium) who, like so many people in the 18th century, was interested in new knowledge (and new merchandise), bought a copy of the anthology for his library and affixed his *ex libris* to it. That book somehow ended up in Southern France, where it remained well preserved, perhaps because no one there could read Dutch. It ultimately found its way to a bric-à-brac market, where it was discovered, somewhat coincidentally, by a resident of Amstelveen

---

76 This is written in the rather complex opening sentence of his logbook — thus in a prominent place. Referring to Psalm 107 verses 23–30, Eyks gives a religious justification for the notion that seamen should relate their disastrous experiences, so that others can learn and benefit from them.

77 Okke de Jong describes a good example of this way of working in the Epilogue to *Shipbreuk in Bengalen* [Shipwreck in Bengal] (2006).

78 As a *maandstukje*, a set of one or more stories for subscribers to a monthly series. It is not certain that Eyks' account was first circulated and then included in the collection of stories. Because the collection was published a relatively short time after his return, it is possible that his story was characterised as a *maandstukje* and only distributed in book form. It is also very possible that the publisher assisted Eyks with the editing of the introduction, considering the solemn style of the opening sentence. Jeroen van der Sande was a prominent member of his church congregation in Middelburg.

during a holiday trip in 1997. He bought the book as a curiosity, even though the story that had 'AMSTELVEEN' in its title was not about the place where he lived, but about a mysterious accident involving an East Indiaman belonging to the VOC, and an onerous, gruelling journey through a barren wilderness. I was lucky enough to be asked to analyse the shipwreck and to be given the opportunity to write a book about the men's survival journey along the desert coast. So, this is how the story went, and in this case even … how one book led to another.

Cornelis Eyks, a life at sea

Little is known about Cornelis Eyks' life and next of kin. On 17 May 1940, in the first week of the Second World War, a large part of the municipal archives of Middelburg went up in flames during an enemy bombardment.[79] The archives had contained the personal details of many of the city's residents, which had been recorded in registers of births, baptisms and marriages; and most likely included the details of Cornelis Eyks and his family. Almost nothing is left of these records, with the exception of the burial registers that record dates of death, and sometimes also details of family relationships. These archives do not contain any information about Eyks, however, because he died in Asia.[80] From these sources, therefore, which normally provide answers to such questions in the Netherlands, we will never know when he was born, or who his parents were.

The personnel records of the VOC, which are still to be found in the Company's archives in The Hague, do contain information on the crew members' places of origin, but not the dates of birth that would allow us to calculate their ages and trace their family relationships. We must therefore be satisfied with the information about Eyks' life as a seaman that can be found in the VOC Archives, which are housed in the National Archives of the Netherlands.

Eyks sailed from Vlissingen to Batavia in the Malay Archipelago five times, but returned only four times. His first voyage on the *Vosmaar*[81] commenced on 29 October 1747, and lasted almost a year. The outward voyage was absolutely disastrous: 94 of the 200 on board died. Eyks had a lucky escape.

Eyks started his career at sea as an ordinary seaman, most likely in 1747. When signing up as a member of the crew, he must have been about fourteen or fifteen years old. From this, we can speculate that he was born around 1733, and was thus about 30 or 31 years old when the *Amstelveen* ran aground in 1763.

79 The parental home on Kraanstraat, from which his mother and sister(s) were buried, met with the same fate. That particular street does not even exist anymore.
80 A rough biography can still be reconstructed. It is known, for instance, that his mother was named Catharina van Ekelen. She lived in Middelburg and died on 27 October 1781. Who his father was remains uncertain. He probably died around 1760. Eyks had one or more sisters, maybe also a brother. It is likely that he did not marry, and as far we know, he had no descendants. He died early in January 1769 in Ceylon (Colombo).
81 The *Vosmaar* was just as old as the *Amstelveen*, but was built in Middelburg. Eyks could follow the construction from nearby and probably worked on the rigging and supplying of the ship. Both ships lay in the roadstead of the Cape of Good Hope in the same time.

58 – The roadstead of Flushing. Engraving by J.C. Philips after C. Pronk, Tirion, 1743

Eyks' experience as a seaman can be derived from his service record, which has been preserved in the VOC Archives in The Hague. Table 1 gives an overview of his outward and homeward-bound voyages in the service of the VOC.

Table 1 – The outward and homeward-bound voyages of Cornelis Eyks

Voyage	Ship / Built in	Departure	Arrival	Rank/Duration of voyage	Captain
1. Outwd	Vosmaar 1746	Rammekens 29-10-1747	Batavia 15-10-1748	Junior seaman 11.5 months	Willem van der Heyden
Return	Vosmaar	Batavia 22-12-1748	Rammekens 15-07-1749	Junior seaman 7.5 months	Willem van der Heyden
2. Outwd	Anna 1741	Rammekens 31-08-1749	Batavia 23-04-1750	Seaman 7.8 months	Jakob Regnault
Return	Woitkensdorp 1739	Ceylon 01-02-1751	Texel 15-09-1751	Seaman 7.5 months	Kornelis Leempoel
3. Outwd	Huis ten Donk 1745	Rammekens 29-01-1752	Batavia 26-07-1752	Seaman 6.0 months	Huibert Vijs
Return	Scholtenburg 1753	Cape 19.02-1760	Goeree 13.06-1760	Gun servant 3.8 months	Pieter Schoneman
4. Outwd	Nw Nieuwerkerk 1749	Rammekens 05-08-1761	Batavia 18-05-1762	Third mate 9.2 months	Adriaan van den Boer
Return	Zuid-Beveland 1755	Batavia 30-10-1765	Rammekens 18-05-1766	Third mate 7.5 months	Huibrecht van der Kneu
5. Outwd	Adm. De Ruyter 1749	Rammekens 17-01-1767	Ceylon 12-12-1767	Third mate 10.9 months	Kornelis van der Putte

Information taken from the website http://vocopvarenden.nationaalarchief.nl, run by the National Archives of the Netherlands in The Hague. Note that detailed information concerning the fourth voyage (during which the *Amstelveen* was lost) is presented in table 2.

This overview shows that in his younger days, Eyks made two voyages to Java. The first was a return voyage to Batavia, while the second was followed by a return voyage via Galle in Ceylon, this time officially recorded as the port of departure. Between the two voyages, Eyks spent only six weeks in Middelburg.

After a four-and-a-half month stay in Middelburg, the third outward voyage marked the start of Eyks' first long-term contract period in Asia, from 1752 to 1760. We know little about this time, with one exception: an adventurous expedition at the beginning of Eyks' homeward-bound voyage with the *Scholtenburg*. This ship arrived at the Cape of Good Hope on 11 March 1759, but sailed two months later, on 7 May 1759, together with the hooker *Hector*, to the Bay of Delagoa, on the eastern coast of the Cape area. There the *Naarstigheid*, coming from Bengal in stormy weather, had been abandoned and set on fire by the crew in July 1757, due to the deplorable condition of the ship. The *Scholtenburg* and the *Hector* took over the cargo of the *Naarstigheid* between 16 June and 6 September 1759, and returned to the Cape on 28 September 1759. There, a few members of crew were accused of stealing and smuggling goods from the *Naarstigheid*. After a long legal investigation, the *Scholtenburg* departed in February 1760 for the Netherlands. The ship anchored in the roadstead of Goeree. In this way, Eyks arrived in Rotterdam. He had been away for a long time, and stayed much longer in Zeeland than he had previously done; almost fourteen months. One can only speculate about the reasons for this long period of leave.

Eyks' second long-term contract period, for the first time as third mate, started with the fourth outward journey. After arriving in Batavia, he first made one or two voyages to Coromandel on the *Nieuw-Nieuwerkerk*. A year later, again back in Batavia, he was transferred to the *Amstelveen* to take a cargo of sugar to Kharg. As we know, this voyage was to end in disaster, and we owe his logbook to that sad event. His *Notes* give us an informal, insider's view of the VOC's trading activities in this part of Asia, and an account of what could happen to the Company's seafaring servants when something went wrong with a ship.

In his journal, the shipping trade is described after Eyks arrived in Muscat with the first castaways. Muscat's harbour was extremely busy. Four large ships were anchored in the roadstead and the day after Eyks arrived, a local trading fleet departed for Kharg. Eyks did not see this fleet until he was on board of one of these ships on his way to meet Buschman. Somewhere in the Gulf — during a period when there was not a breath of wind — he hailed a ship belonging to the English East India Company, which was bound for Bengal. He was received on the ship in a most friendly manner, and invited by the captain to sail with them with free board to Madras. Presumably out of a sense of duty, Eyks did not take up this tempting offer. Other survivors of the shipwreck, including Jonas Daalberg, were pleased to sail in this way to Bengal. Nearly all the seamen who did not sail with Eyks by way of Kharg joined passing English ships to India, and from there, VOC ships to Batavia. This show of courtesy contrasts sharply with the ideas and attitude of Batavia at the time. The High Government feared the English in Gamron and demanded compensation from them for losses, following the destruction of the Company's warehouse there. Batavia even ordered the VOC's employees to keep their distance from other citizens of other nations. The Resident of Kharg, for instance, was forbidden by the High Government from delivering goods such as sailcloth and caulking cotton to foreign ships, except in emergencies.

Eyks travelled as a passenger on one of the freighters belonging to the Arabian trading fleet, and thereby got to learn about other aspects of Asian merchant shipping on the way to Kharg, as described above. He clearly indicates that his presence in the fleet had an influence on the actions of the distrustful captains from Sur, Muscat and Sohar, and ultimately resulted in the prevention of a skirmish. That was an entirely different contribution to good relations from, for example, the courteous but rather obsequious letter (inv. no. 3156), that Batavia wrote to the Governor of Bandar Abbasi in connection with the attack on the former VOC warehouse there:

The Governor General Petrus Albertus van der Parra and the Councillors of Dutch East India send this letter of friendship in reply to the letter from their friend, His Serene Highness Jaffer Chan, Governor of Bandar Abbasi (or Gamron).

It has extremely disconcerted and affected us that servants of the English Company attacked the native village Abbasi, which resulted in some of Your Excellency's subordinates losing their lives and much of their property.
On this occasion we have again seen a token of the affection which Your Excellency continues to show the Dutch East India Company by having our warehouse guarded, which has suffered substantially from the riots, because the merchants who had taken shelter there were attacked by the English, who shattered doors, windows and other woodwork of that warehouse.
We thank Your Excellency for this proven protection and will not fail on any occasion to acknowledge this friendliness [favour].
Our desire is not less than that of Your Excellency to restart the discontinued trade with Your Excellency and subjects and to have it continue as before, but Your Excellency certainly understands that the war still raging in the inland of the [Persian] Empire, and the riots at the borders of that Empire have caused such a dearth of custom that, only with much effort and inducement can one market one or two shiploads on Kharg, apart from the exposure to disturbances by bandits roaming about here and there.
Should it happen, however, that an end comes to that war and the other uncertain circumstances, we shall devote the necessary attention to Your Excellency's proposal, because the success of that revival [of trade] will, after all, be of benefit to the Company as well as Your Excellency.
In the meantime, we wish Your Excellency lasting health, a long life and a prosperous Government.

Written in Castle Batavia on the Island of Great Java on 18 May 1764. The Governor General of Dutch East India, signed by P. van der Parra; with seal imprinted in red wax on the side [...], and signed by ordinance by Jan Willem Falck, Secretary.

The object and tone of this letter illustrate the evident distance between the activities of the High Government in Batavia and ordinary seamen, whose lot was simply to try and survive in the extremely demanding situations that occasionally faced them in the course of their normal seafaring duties. The letter mentions some subordinates (the author of the letter may have meant 'subjects') who had died during the attack on the warehouse in Gamron. As far as can be ascertained, the High Government in Batavia never expressed similar concern about the fate of the 75 drowned seamen of the *Amstelveen*.

One cannot fail to note another striking fact. Resident Buschman sent Eyks and the boatswain's mate away without any employment. The boatswain's mate subsequently died on the way to Batavia. In Batavia, the VOC officials *knew* that Pieter van Holland had survived the disaster. Seven weeks' pay was nevertheless posthumously withheld from his relatives in his homeland by terminating his employment on 15 June 1763, the date of departure, instead of on 7 August 1763, the day the *Amstelveen* was lost. As a result of Buschman's decision, Eyks was not re-employed until 18 June 1764 (almost eleven months later), even though he was not blamed for the accident during the interrogation in Batavia. Nor was Buschman blamed for anything, and his decision was not revoked. Eyks was thus neither rewarded for the exemplary performance of his duties after the disaster, nor compensated for loss of income. In short, everything was settled greedily 'for the benefit of the Company' by some gentlemen in velvet with little eye for the risks and consequences of ocean-going merchant shipping for those who put their modest possessions — and even their lives — in jeopardy for the work they had to do.

On the other hand, as a consequence of the letter from Batavia to the Governor of Gamron, Buschman had again received a clear reminder of Company policy. Batavia ordered him to recover the financial loss from the English and 'to aver every conceivable courtesy and friendliness towards the Duke, as well as the other dignitaries in the Gulf, without harming the Company, and without getting involved in their mutual disputes or those of the English.'

Certainly, the English captains who picked up the helpless, hungry survivors in Muscat would never have received a similar letter of thanks from Batavia.

Table 2 gives an overview of Eyks' Asian voyages during his fourth contract period (his second long-term contract), from his outward voyage on 5 August 1761 to his return to Zeeland, safe and sound, on 18 May 1766.

Table 2 – Eyks' travels during his fourth contract (incl. outward and homeward voyages)

Voyage	Ship/ Built in	Departure/ Date	Arrival/ Date	Position/ Status	Captain/ master
4a.	Nieuw-Nieuwerkerk 1749	Rammekens 05-08-1761	Batavia 18-05-1762	Third mate	Adriaan van den Boer
4b.	Idem	Batavia Dates missing	Coromandel Dates missing	Third mate	Idem
4c.	Amstelveen 1746	Batavia 16-06-1763	Wrecked 05/07-08-1763	Third mate	Nicolaas Pietersen
4d.	Ships of local merchants	Hadd / Sur 07-09-1753	Matra (Muscat) 10-09-1763	Shipwrecked seaman	Arabian merchants
4e.	Arabian trading fleet	Muscat 13-09-1763	Kharq 03-10-1763	Passenger	Arabian merchants
4f.	De Courier (priv. ship)	Kharq 19-10-'63 Muscat 11/18-12-'63	Cochin 22-01-1764	Transported unemployed	N. Lasboom
4g.	Erf-Prins 1750	Cochin 31-03-1764	Batavia	Transported unemployed	P. Schoneman
			22-05-1764	Doing duties for a living	
			18-06-1764	Re-employed by the VOC	
4h.	Lekkerland 1753	Batavia 30-06-1764 Muscat 25/31-08-'64	Kharq 11-10-1764	Third mate	Christiaan Blom
4i.	Idem	Kharq 03-11-1764	Batavia 02-04-1765	Third mate	Christiaan Blom
4j.	Idem	Batavia 04-05-1765	Cheribon v.v. 12-06-1765	Third mate	Christiaan Blom
4k.	Zuid-Beveland 1755	Batavia 30-10-1765	Rammekens 18-05-1766	Third mate	Huibrecht van der Kneu

Sources: Eyk's *Notes* and the website http://vocopvarenden.nationaalarchief.nl.

Seven months later, Eyks set out again for the East Indies. His fifth contract was charged with a *maandbrief* (an agreement concerning the regular payment of part of his wages) in favour of his mother,[82] Catharina van Ekelen. This had not been the case for his previous voyages. Had his father perhaps died at the beginning of the 1760s, during Eyks' unusually long leave, prior to his fourth East Indies voyage?

Just like several other survivors of the disaster, Cornelis Eyks died within a few years of their adventure on the desert coast of Oman. He passed away on 16 January 1769, in or near Ceylon (Sri Lanka), and was buried in Colombo. His

82 In this contract, Eyks' mother was named, which proved a crucial finding in our genealogical search.

estate was auctioned there, and his liabilities were deducted from the proceeds. On 26 May 1771, the remainder of the *maandbrief* was settled with his mother. Subsequently, on 11 August 1775, a further sum was paid to the Consignations Office (*Comptoir van Consignatiën*) in Middelburg, presumably to compensate the costs of her benefit from the Zeeland Widow Fund. She died on 27 October 1781.

Causes and location of the disaster

It is still not entirely clear why the *Amstelveen* ran aground so unexpectedly at Cape Mataraca. We know the immediate cause: an error in the interpretation of an observation on board. How could this have happened? The crew saw land in the distance, diagonally behind them, and assumed that this was the coast of the Cape that they had been looking for; in other words, they assumed that they saw Cape Mataraca behind them. Captain Pietersen was particularly convinced of this, but his self-assurance was unwarranted. In the evening, less than half a day later, the ship ran aground in fog and darkness on the low, broad beach of that cape.

What *had* they seen, and how could they have been so terribly mistaken? At about 12 noon at lat. 18° 40' N, they had sailed much closer to the coast than they thought. They did see land in the distance, but not the broad beach in between, which was closer and totally hidden from view by the fog. In front of them, Cape Mataraca was apparently also completely covered by fog. The ship, meanwhile, sailed in beautifully clear weather. The bright sun, first in the east and then gradually by way of the south to the southwest, shed glaring incident light on the ground fog. At a distance, it is often difficult to distinguish bright sunlight on low-hanging fog from sunlit water, as long as the light is shining fully on it.

In the distance, diagonally behind them, some peaks of high cliffs stood out above the low-hanging fog, producing an optical illusion of coastland. These cliffs are properly noted in modern nautical charts of that area,[83] but that was not the case for the nautical chart used on board the *Amstelveen*. This explains why, on a good course, the ship ran aground suddenly that evening on the coast of the Cape, which the crew thought they had already passed many hours ago.

Were they really not to blame for anything? The captain sailed with bravura, aided by a chart that was ill-suited to the manner of navigation he seems to have preferred: sailing in sight of the coast. Despite this, they went ahead, guided by a chart and sailing directives whose reliability could not be gauged.

---

83 Looking west-south-west from the poop, they saw the cliffs of Al Ask. These are 150 metres high on average, 120 metres higher than the land between these cliffs and the sea. These expansive cliffs are located approximately 20 km inland at lat. 18° 37' N and long. 56° 30' E. The peak (Funnel Hill) is 180 m high, and is located somewhat more to the south and farther inland.

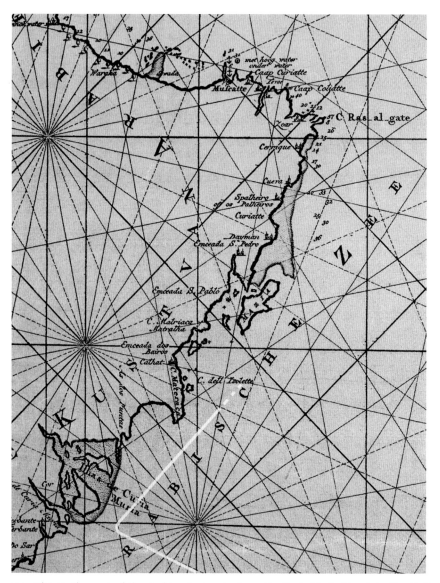

59 – The south coast of the Arabian Peninsula, from the Curia Muria Islands to the Gulf of Oman, with Cape Mataraca, Mazia (Masirah) and Ras al Gate (Hadd). Part of a map of the Arabian Sea by Johannes van Keulen (1754). The *Amstelveen* sailed to this coast in accordance with the VOC's sailing instructions, from the equator south of the Maldiven Islands in a north-westerly direction. Two independent sources (Eyks' *Notes* and a VOC report concerning the interrogation of two seamen from the *Amstelveen* who happened to reach Negapatnam in India) reported that in the afternoon, the ship had sailed at a latitude of 18°, and that she had stuck to this course in the SW monsoon. No land could be seen. At sunset, the captain changed his course to the north-east, so as to reach the entrance to the Persian Gulf as soon as possible. That course, obviously safe for sailing at night, is illustrated in white on this map (which they most probably used on board). As we now know, the position of the Curia Muria Islands on the map (south of latitude 18°) is erroneous, as is the downward-curving coastline of Cape Mataraca. As in many other old maps, however, the eastern part of the cape is drawn correctly at about latitude 19°.

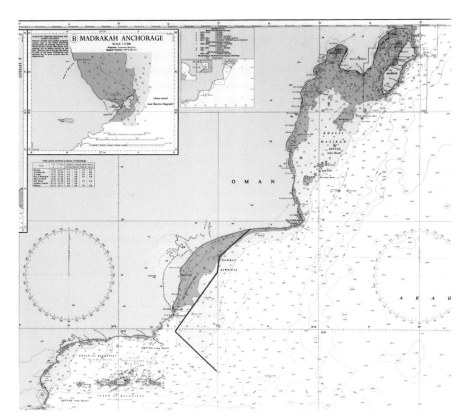

60 – A much smaller part of the south coast of Oman on a modern sea chart. To the south-west of Ras Madrakah (Cape Mataraca) is Al Hallaniyat (the Curia Muria Islands) and the huge Sawqirah Bay; and to the north, Khalij Masirah (the Gulf of Masirah, Enzaädades Baixos) and Masirah Island. Part of chart BA 3785, *Arabia, Oman, Port Salalah to Masirah*, British Admiralty, 2001. The red line shows what really happened on Friday, 5 August 1763. The night of 4/5 August, the *Amstelveen* sailed much closer to the coast than was presumed on board. The next morning at 9 p.m. they saw coastland in the distance and an almost northerly course was chosen, to get more coastland in sight. At noon the captain decided to turn again to a north-easterly course, presuming that the coastland they saw abaft the beam was Cape Mataraca, and that it should soon disappear behind the horizon. From the topmast nothing could be seen to the north. In the afternoon, they still saw coastland in the distance, and soon after in the darkness, nothing could be seen. They expected to see Masirah the next morning, but ran aground that evening in an unknown location.

In fact, VOC ships never went so far south: they normally had to sail to the Arabian coast much farther to the north, and stay much farther from the coast.

So as to have more land in sight, after 9 o'clock in the morning, the captain changed his north-easterly course to north by east, a more northerly direction. This was wrong, risky and, above all, unnecessary. In his logbook, Eyks characterised this change of course as 'audacious' [*stoutelijk*].

Furthermore, Captain Pietersen ignored a number of observations that seriously worried the others: an eastern-longitude measurement showing that they were hugging the coast; the presence of cormorants (which usually look for food in shallow waters); and increasingly higher waves in a moderate wind, which was not in keeping with the height of the waves. The captain did not want to take soundings, however: in his view, the ship was no longer strong enough to withstand the high waves coming from behind.

On the poop, no one viewed the waves as an effect of long monsoon undulation in shallow water; in fact, they were breakers. Slot (1993) has rightly pointed out that it was odd that Captain Pietersen, from Husum near the German Bay in the North Sea, known for its perilous breakers, did not perceive them in this way. He of all people should have been aware of this. This is an observation that one could also apply to the other navigators on board the *Amstelveen*.

Moreover, for some reason, Captain Pietersen was in a hurry. He felt sure of himself — perhaps too sure — and, after deciding not to sound, did not deviate to the east for certainty's sake. Surely he must have realised that they would soon be in deeper water then and the swell would become calmer again, if they had indeed unintentionally ended up in shallow water. Apparently he neither received nor tolerated objections. Perhaps the fact that the ship lacked a fully authorised, experienced first mate — as may well have been the case — took its toll in the end.

Exactly what happened that evening is difficult to fathom. No sounding was taken while there was no wind. The captain had indeed recommended doing so at the transfer of the watch to the first mate, but it is not easy to sound in the dark with strong breakers; indeed, it is very dangerous, because of the rolling of the ship. Somewhat later, it was already too late, and after a day and a half, the waves shattered the old, lopsided ship. While it is true that soundings were not taken because of the poor condition of the ship, the risk involved had not been recognised, and was not lessened by a change in the course to a more easterly direction. Captain Pietersen was in too much of a hurry, and too convinced that he was right.

Anyone who measures a distance of 45 km at lat. 18° 40' N on a modern nautical chart from the cliffs of Al Ask and from there, plots a route to the north-east, will end up on the south coast of Cape Mataraca. The *Amstelveen* ran aground somewhere near that coast, perhaps somewhat more to the east because of the current along the coast. To use the language of an octant: at approximately lat. 18° 56' N and long. 57° 25' E. She got stuck on a rocky sandbank in about 20 feet (6 metres) of deep water, 250 years ago, along an almost uncharted coast that may have changed significantly since.[84]

---

84 In the Maldives, the coral has grown 2.5 to 3 metres in height since the middle of the 18th century. (R. Paesie, 1999, p. 17–19).

Those on board and their fate

The *Amstelveen* was wrecked during a voyage in Asia. Until recently, it was almost impossible to trace the fate of the crew of a VOC ship on such a voyage. The personnel records of the Company were not designed for this. On departure, the Captain received a copy of the muster roll, but that of the *Amstelveen* was lost when the ship ran aground.[85] Thanks to the recent digitisation of parts of the huge VOC archives at The Hague, it has become possible to trace the fates of most of the crew of the *Amstelveen*. This is only possible for voyages that ended in shipwreck with many victims, as the employment contracts of the dead were then terminated and the name of the wrecked ship was recorded. The names of the dead can be traced on http://vocopvarenden.nationaalarchief.nl, allowing us to reconstruct the core of the muster roll.

Thirty members of crew survived the accident on the *Amstelveen*. The muster by Jonas Daalberg on Cape Mataraca provided the personal details of five crew members. Afterwards, Eyks mentioned a few more seamen's names in his logbook. Furthermore, in Batavia, the names of two more seamen turned up; men who had sailed to Madras on an English ship and were interrogated in Nagapatnam. In that way, nineteen of the 30 castaways could ultimately be identified. The information from the Company's archives and that on the survivors was then compared, revealing that some additional corrections needed to be made. For instance, Pieter Coene, the bay man, did not die when the ship ran aground on Cape Mataraca, but some four weeks later from illness and exhaustion near Hadd.

Table 3 gives the results of this complex search, including the corrections. The left-hand columns together constitute the reconstructed muster roll. In the right-hand columns, the reasons for termination of employment or the fate of the survivors after the ship ran aground are given. The third column lists the 85 crew members of the Amstelveen as well as 20 military men by their position (occupation and/or rank). The group of military men bound for Kareek counted 18 soldiers and two officers. This column includes, however, also 27 bosschieters (translated as gun servants). In fact, these men are civilians: senior members of the crew, who have experience and can also operate the ship's cannons. They are higher ranked, somewhat better paid seamen (see p. 101).

---

85 Buschman wrote to Batavia on 5 October 1763 that 'all papers' had been lost. The original muster roll might still be in the VOC archives in Batavia.

Table 3 – Those on board the *Amstelveen* and their fates after the shipwreck on 5 August 1763

Name	Origin	Position	Reason for end of employment	Details fate of survivors
a. From the VOC Archives				
Nicolaas **Anderlecks**	Canton Bern	Soldier	Last mentioned	15-06-1763
Joris **Asmus**	Dendermonde	Gun servant	Last mentioned	15-06-1763
Douwe **Baukes**	Sneek	Corporal	End employmt	15-06-1763
Hendrik **Blaas**	Heeren	Soldier	End employmt	15-06-1763
Jan Pieter **Beekman**	Bremen	Third Mate	Last mentioned	15-06-1763
Jochem **Berghout**	Wismar	Gun servant	Ship wrecked	
Hans Daniël **Berkman**	Hamburg	Gun servant	Ship wrecked	
Simon **Bijslij**	Dettingen	Gun servant	Ship wrecked	
Joseph **Cambier**	Ghent	Soldier	End employmt	07-08-1763
Cornelis **Caspersse**	Stralsund	Gun servant	Ship wrecked	
Johannes **Coenen**	Prussia	Soldier	End employmt	15-06-1763
Louis **Colo**	Paris	Soldier	Ship wrecked	
Jan **Cristiaansse**	Cologne	Gun servant	Ship wrecked	
Johan Christoffel **Crouse**	Leijdenberg	Soldier	Ship wrecked	
Gerrit van **Dijk**	Amersfoort	Seaman	Ship wrecked	
Johan **Dominiconi**	Livorno	Seaman	Ship wrecked	
Johannes **Douwes**	Franeker	Junior Seaman	Ship wrecked	
Matthijs **Eegakker**	Kleijnekemps	Barrelmaker	End employmt	15-06-1763
Franciscus **Feurle**	Genoa	Seaman	Ship wrecked	
Matthijs **Fortenberg**	Frankfort /Oder	Junior Seaman	Ship wrecked	
Johan **Gerink**	Cleves	Junior Seaman	Last mentioned	15-06-1763
Peeter Hendrik **Geuvert**	Bielefeld	Soldier	Ship wrecked	
Roulott **Hanssen**	Edam	Apprentice	Ship wrecked	
Frans **Harla**	Delft	Steward	Ship wrecked	
Claas **Hasselaer**	Groningen	Seaman	Ship wrecked	
Pieter **Hellendaan**	Nijmegen	Soldier	Ship wrecked	
Mattias **Herkenraet**	Keulen	Seaman	Ship wrecked	
Jochem **Herps**	Stettin	Gun servant	Ship wrecked	
Aernoudt van **Hoding**	Leiden	Seaman	Ship wrecked	
Jan **Jacobs**	Laaglandlist	Seaman	Ship wrecked	
Hendrik **Jansen**	Groningen	Ship's Corporal	Ship wrecked	
Harmen **Jaspers**	Hopsen	Gun servant	Ship wrecked	
Dirk Pieterse **Keijser**	Ilpendam	Seaman	Ship wrecked	
Willem **Klijn**	Kassel/Hessen	Apprentice	Ship wrecked	
Claas **Kommerou**	Drachten	Seaman	Ship wrecked	
Jan Jacob **Koning**	Danzig	Gun servant	Ship wrecked	
Dirk **Kroese**	The Hague	Seaman	Ship wrecked	
Jan **Kuijpers**	Bremen	2nd Boatswain	Ship wrecked	
Andries **Laurens**	Flensburg	Chief Sailmaker	Ship wrecked	
Willem **Lemmes**	Copenhagen	Gun servant	Ship wrecked	
Johannes **Loblans**	Amersfoort	Junior Seaman	Last mentioned	15-06-1763
Christiaen **Man**	Brunswijk	Gun servant	Ship wrecked	
Andries **Marre**	Strassbourg	Soldier	End employmt	15-06-1763
Geert **Mennes**	Leems	Gun servant	End employmt	15-06-1763
Johan Andries **Milder**	Amspach	Junior Soldier	Ship wrecked	

Name	Origin	Position	Reason for end of employment	Details fate of survivors
Jan Laurens **Minikener**	Livorno	Gun servant	Ship wrecked	
Christoffel **Muller**	Etling	Junior Seaman	Ship wrecked	
Gerrit **Nieuwmans**	Amsterdam	Seaman	Ship wrecked	
Jan **Nuij**	Amsterdam	Gun servant	Ship wrecked	
Jan van **Oorschot**	The Hague	Magistrate	Ship wrecked	
Jonas **Orre**	Karlskrona	Third Mate	Ship wrecked	
Nicolaas **Pietersen**	Husum	Captain/Master	Ship wrecked	
Hendrik **Plets**	Venlo	Seaman	Ship wrecked	
Jan **Redeker**	Amsterdam	Junior Seaman	Ship wrecked	
Pieter **Roeding**	Zwolle	Soldier	Last mentioned	15-06-1763
Jan van **Ruijven**	Arnhem	Gun servant	Ship wrecked	
Andries v. **Scherpenzeel**	The Hague	Seaman	Ship wrecked	
Matthijs **Schoenmaker**	Bremen	Gun servant	Ship wrecked	
Johannes Dirkse **Schoor**	Wormerveer	Junior Seaman	Ship wrecked	
Jan Jurriaan **Schoover**	Hessen	Soldier	Last mentioned	15-06-1763
Salvo **Schorvinack**	Naples	Seaman	Last mentioned	15-06-1763
Jan **Schreuder**	Husum	Third Mate	Ship wrecked	
Reijnt **Sijmons**	Groningen	Gun servant	Ship wrecked	
Leendert van **Silva**	Corhem	Junior Seaman	Ship wrecked	
Johan George **Sjouwer**	Rodenburg	Soldier	Ship wrecked	
Hendrik **Slegt**	Vreede	Junior Seaman	Ship wrecked	
Hendrik **Smits**	Haarlem	Seaman	Ship wrecked	
Jan Babtist **Snijder**	Antwerp	Soldier	Last mentioned	15-06-1763
Coenraadt **Steijn**	Osnabrück	Soldier	Ship wrecked	
Marten **Stekeling**	Colberg	Boatswain's mt.	Ship wrecked	
Isaak **Sterk**	Amsterdam	Boy	Ship wrecked	
Arie **Stobben**	Amsterdam	Gun servant	Ship wrecked	
Gerrit **Tenhouten**	Amsterdam	Surgeon	Last mentioned	15-06-1763
Cornelis **Uijl**	Renbimnen	Gun servant	Ship wrecked	
Jan Jacob **Veltboom**	Bern	Soldier	Ship wrecked	
Hendrik **Vrindt**	Schagen	Apprentice	Ship wrecked	
Hendrik **Wassink**	Alten	Cook	Last mentioned	15-06-1763
Steve **Weesing**	Amsterdam	Carpenter's mate	Ship wrecked	
Augusteijn **Weks**	Elingen	Soldier	Last mentioned	05-08-1763
Jan van der **Werff**	Noordwijk	Gun servant	Last mentioned	15-06-1763
Roeloff **Wesloff**	Westerwijk	Chief gunner	Ship wrecked	
Hendrik **Wetters**	Lippstadt	Boy	Last mentioned	15-06-1763
Pankras **Wijtvelt**	Amsterdam	Gun servant	Ship wrecked	
Evert **Willemsse**	Kampen	Gun servant	Ship wrecked	
Pieter **Wip**	Amsterdam	Seaman	Ship wrecked	
Subtotal	85 including 11 anonymous survivors.* 1 first mate, name unknown			
In total	74 dead. Plus: a mystery. In total 75 dead.			

* It was not possible to trace the eleven anonymous survivors using the VOC records. The dates for the termination of employment for two crew members are correct. This suggests that they might have been among the group of eleven anonymous survivors.

Name	Origin	Position	Details fate of survivors
b. From Eyks' logbook (survivors)			
Jacobus Joh. **Balthazar**	Wetteren	Apprentice	Completed the walk / Kharg
Jan **Brinkhuijs**	Amsterdam	Gun servant	Arrived / Nagapatnam
Barend **Bronkhorst**	Batavia	Ord. seaman	1-yr journey, died on 16-1-1767
Pieter **Coene**	Middelburg	Bayman	Died during the walk
Jonas **Daalberg**	Tonsberg	Boatswain	Died in Ceylon on 29-7-1767
Jan **Drevens**	Appingedam	Gun servant	Died during the walk
Cornelis **Eyks**	Middelburg	Third mate	Died in Ceylon on 15-1-1769
Pieter van **Holland**	Rotterdam	Boatswain's m.	Died on board Erf-prins
Steven **Hillekens**	Deventer	Ord. Seaman	Walked to Muscat / Batavia
Matthys **Janszen**	Danzig	Seaman	Completed the walk / Kharg
Jacob **Kleijn**	Amsterdam?	Seaman	Survived the walk / unknown
Andries **Kolstrop**	Drontheim	Gun servant	Completed the walk / Kharg
Hans **Lutjens**	Hamburg	Asst. Cook	Dropped out 19-8-'63; died?
Willem **Nicolson**	Hertogenbosch	Gun servant	Completed the walk / Kharg
Carsten **Pietersze**	Heir / Huijer	Gun servant	Completed the walk / Kharg
Hendrik **Poolman**	Hamburg	Seaman	Arrived / Nagapatnam
Cornelis de **Reus**	Blijswijk	Seaman	De Geus? Completed the walk
Jan **Teunisse**	Luxembourg	Seaman	Completed the walk / Kharg
Little Javanese Boy	Batavia	Boy (slave)	Abducted by Bedouin 23-8-'63
Subtotal	19 Survivors, identity known; and 11 Survivors, not identified; total 30 survivors on 07-08-1763. First mate, name unknown		In total 74 dead. Plus: a mystery. In total 75 dead.
In total	75 dead + 30 survivors = 105 persons		

One can gather from this overview that the men on board the *Amstelveen* came from all over Europe.[86] Half of them came from the Netherlands, a third from Germany, and the remainder from Belgium, Luxembourg, France, Switzerland, Italy, Denmark, Norway and Sweden. In a few cases the men's origins could not be traced, mainly because of the unclear phonetic notation used during signing up in the Netherlands.

The identity of the first mate could not be traced during the reconstruction of the muster roll.[87] Neither could the eleven anonymous castaways in the

86 There is only one exception: the little Javanese slave boy. His presence on board has not been documented in the VOC Archives.

87 Table 3 shows that there were four navigators on board with the rank of third mate. One of them, Jan Schreuder, had already sailed as third mate on the outward voyage of the *Amstelveen* to Batavia and apparently stayed on board there. On the outward voyage, he may have replaced the first mate, Hendrik Wijnboom, who fell ill under way and died in Batavia, a situation that may have continued during the voyage to Kharg. Just like Captain Pietersen, Jan Schreuder came from Hussum. He presumably knew the ship well, because he had already sailed her during the third return voyage of the *Amstelveen* as a gun servant. However, there is no direct evidence to support this. Both of the other 'old navigators'

group of 30 survivors that left for Muscat on 11 August 1763 be identified in the VOC Archives. Eyks wrote that 22 men had arrived safe and sound in Muscat. These included some of the men from this anonymous group of survivors, but their names could not be traced.

In the records of the VOC, three terms were used to indicate that a person on board had died and that his employment had been terminated: 'shipwrecked,' 'last mentioned' and 'date of end of employment.' In the case of the *Amstelveen*, the date of departure from Batavia was often chosen as the date on which payment ended. This was clearly unjust, as Eyks and Buschman had reported the correct date of the accident immediately. While withholding seven weeks' pay was clearly profitable for the Company, the surviving relatives were wronged; not only were they denied wages that they were owed, but they were apparently also misled as to the date and circumstances of the accident.

The question as to whether or not a first mate was indeed on board could not be answered directly by searching the VOC Archives. It is, however, just one of the remaining mysteries, which we will now deal with briefly in conclusion.

[Dutch: '*oude Stuurluij*', mentioned by Eyks in his letter to Mr Buschman] were new on board, as was Eyks himself.

Remaining mysteries

The circumstances surrounding the wreck of the *Amstelveen* have remained a mystery for nearly two-and-a-half centuries. The discovery of Eyks' *Notes*, the logbook as it had been published in 1766, changed this, enabling us to deduce the causes and the location of the disaster. Both the gravity and the consequences of the accident could now finally be understood. The search to find out what happened in Oman on 5 August 1763, and in the weeks and months following the accident, gave rise to many new questions, however, to which no conclusive answers have yet been found. This closing chapter outlines some of these remaining mysteries, both to indicate that further research is needed, and also to provide a starting point for readers who, inspired by this book, would like to try to solve some of the remaining mysteries themselves.

The first such mystery is: why did the ship approach the Arabian Peninsula so prematurely? The *Amstelveen* made a rough but successful ocean crossing. There are no indications that the ship had gone off course unintentionally. On the contrary, Eyks' description of what happened on board and what Captain Pietersen told him at the change of the evening watch about his considerations suggest that the deviation from the usual course was intentional. He emphasised his goal: entering the Persian Gulf as quickly as possible. What, however, induced Captain Pietersen to approach the coast of Oman at 18° N instead of at 22° N, far north of Masirah Island, as was usual and recommended in the sailing directions? Why did he try to hug the dangerous coast so far to the south, knowing that he still had to sail hundreds of miles in the favourable following monsoon wind in a north-easterly direction?

The second mystery concerns the failure to recognise the danger of sailing in possibly shallow water. There had been many alarming indications that the problems facing the captain and crew — unusually high waves, a heavily rolling ship, uncertainty as to the depth of the water — stemmed from an incorrect position, or from the failure to accept the correct readings on the basis of a mistaken sighting of the coast. Instead of seeking deeper water in an easterly direction, they attempted to get more land in sight by taking a more northerly course. The mystery is, of course, why Captain Pietersen, when he thought they could not sound, did not choose a more easterly course for safety's sake, to see if they could sail into deeper, probably calmer water?

The third mystery concerns the identity of the first mate. He is mentioned without any reservation in two independent sources, but in both cases, not by name: in Eyks' logbook (and in his letter to Buschman), and in the account given by the two seamen, Brinkhuijs and Poolman, who were interrogated in Nagapatnam. In the Resolution of the High Government in Batavia, which concluded the investigation of the accident, the principal offenders (the captain and the first mate) were not mentioned by name. With the aid of the website http://vocopvarenden.nationaalarchief.nl, we were able to establish the identity of all the crew members, with the exception of the first mate. It appears, however, that there were not three (as Eyks had written to Buschman) but *four* navigators holding the rank of third mate on board. Did one of them fulfil the role of first mate without having been appointed to it? Was this approved by Batavia, but not entered in the pay book? Why did the captain speak directly to Eyks and give him orders at the transfer of the watch to the first mate? Who was the responsible officer of the watch, and where was he at the time of the accident? In short it remains a mystery who acted as first mate and on what authority.

The fourth mystery concerns the chaos and ineptitude on board the stranded ship, both on the night she ran aground and in the morning, when it was possible to survey and assess the situation. Not a word is written in the logbook about consultation or initiatives involving the officers, or about the leadership that should come from the captain in such a perilous situation. Everyone realised that the usual life-saving devices were inadequate, while it seemed possible to bridge the distance to the coast. The only man to keep a cool head and set a good example was Jonas Daalberg, the boatswain, who went ashore on a spar, together with an experienced seaman. Everyone saw it from nearby, but no rescue plan was made for crew members who could not count on a place in the longboat. Where was the captain, and what did he do to prevent the disaster that was looming?

The fifth mystery is Eyks' silence concerning the passenger on board, Jan van Oorschot. That he had most probably been on the ship emerged during the search for the names of those on board in the archives. At first sight, this might not seem particularly relevant to understanding the circumstances of the shipwreck, but it is certainly odd. Jan van Oorschot was the only guest on board. As a judge, he was a high-ranking VOC servant, but neither Eyks nor Batavia made any mention of his presence. It is also odd, not to say remarkable, that his death was not reported to Buschman. The judge was travelling to see him unannounced. Was he indeed on board, and why was he sailing with them?

This mystery was recently solved. According to an entry in the paybook of the *Amstelveen*, Jan van Schagen died in Batavia on 10 June 1763. This entry was not included in the delivery of data for the website http://vocopvarenden. nationaalarchief.nl. In short: the magistrate was not on board. He died in the hospital in Batavia, five or so days prior to the departure of the *Amstelveen*.

The sixth mystery relates to Eyks' frequent silence on matters which initially provoke his readers' curiosity. At various moments, he falls silent on weighty matters, without it being clear why. He does not let slip a word of his opinion of the first mate with whom he kept watch on board. We do not hear anything specific about his visit to Fort Mosselstein, nor about the purpose of his voyage to Kharg. Once in Batavia, he was silent about the reunion with Jonas Daalberg. Did the boatswain avoid him because Eyks had continued without him? Nor does Eyks say anything about his interrogation in Batavia and his treatment by the high-ranking investigators there. Nor do his *Notes* conclude with an evaluation of his experiences in Batavia, as he had done before, for example, near Duqm and during the return voyage to Batavia in the roadstead of Muscat. The mystery is thus: why was Eyks silent until the bitter end on such matters, when being more open would have given the reader a better understanding of his story? Was he hiding something, and if so, what, and why did he do so? Or did he simply obey the general rule that matters of interest to the VOC should be kept secret by employees of the *Edele Compagnie* — the Honourable Company — as the VOC was known in the 18th century?

The seventh mystery concerns what happened on Cape Mataraca after the shipwrecked sailors had left. First the Bedouin would have combed the beach for what they could easily take with them; it was easy to get to the beach by camel. It is likely that the merchant captain from Hadd arrived shortly after the end of the south-westerly monsoon. The port side of the ship with the cannon was lying on the beach; the wreck was accessible. We do not know what he took with him. In Muscat, it was decided to send two ships to the wreck. Narrottam hired a dhow and the Iman of Oman sent a galley with oarsmen. In Muscat, Eyks heard from Narrottam on 11 December 1763 that just one ship had returned with some goods. The anchors were still lying on the beach, and Eyks was told nothing at all about the cannons. The agent's behaviour caused Eyks to become increasingly suspicious. He felt thwarted; in Batavia he could be accused of neglecting his duty because he had not made a record of what had been rescued from the wreck. The mystery is: what was Narrottam trying to hide from Eyks? Why had the anchors not been brought too? And above all: where were the valuable cannons?

Here, too, more details have come to light. James Onley recently revealed (2008, p.84) that since 1758, Narrottam had mainly been serving the English in secret. They paid him as a broker, but he also functioned as an intelligence agent; as a spy, in fact, for the East India Company and the British administrative apparatus in Bombay. He was even praised lavishly by the governor of Bombay in 1763 (sic!): 'the English Broker at Muscat, having on many occasions being very serviceable in transmitting intelligence'. In 1798, however, he was sacked by the governor of Bombay for fraud (Onley, 2008, p.84). He had managed to play his double game for many years, but he got his comeuppance in the end.

'The salvaged people'

On the title page of his *Notes*, Eyks dedicated his logbook to 'the salvaged people of the Dutch East India Company Ship AMSTELVEEN,' without mentioning the survivors by name. He did not yet know all of them, had been unable to note anything down under way, and it was impossible to correct this afterwards. We can only partly make up for this shortcoming here, as eleven survivors still remain anonymous. All of the survivors are listed below as a token of honour:

*Jacobus Johannes Balthazar — Jan Brinkhuijs — Barend Bronkhorst
Pieter Coene — Jonas Daalberg — Jan Drevens — Cornelis Eyks
Steven Hillekens — Pieter van Holland — Matthys Janszen — Jacob Kleyn
Andries Kolstrop — Hans Lutjes — Willem Nicolson — Carsten Pietersze
Hendrik Poolman — Cornelis de Reus — Jan Theunisze
the little Javanese boy — and eleven others (unknown).*

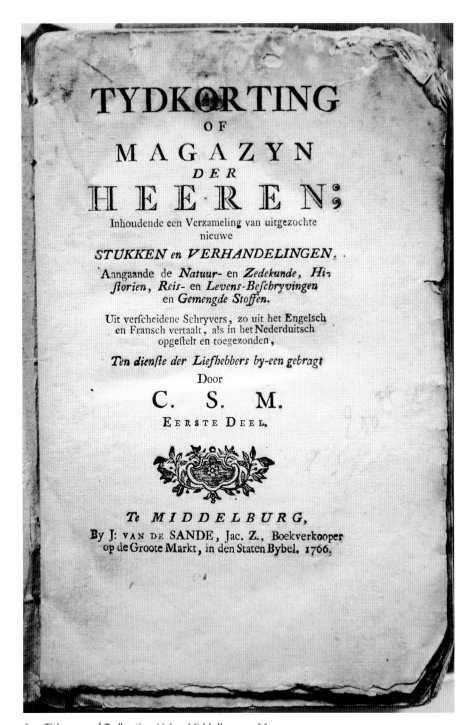

TYDKORTING
OF
MAGAZYN
DER
HEEREN:
Inhoudende een Verzameling van uitgezochte
nieuwe

STUKKEN en VERHANDELINGEN,

Aangaande de *Natuur-* en *Zedekunde, Hi-
storien, Reis-* en *Levens-Beschryvingen*
en *Gemengde Stoffen.*

Uit verscheidene Schryvers, zo uit het Engelsch
en Fransch vertaalt, als in het Nederduitsch
opgestelt en toegezonden,

Ten dienste der Liefhebbers by-een gebragt

Door

C. S. M.
EERSTE DEEL.

Te MIDDELBURG,
By J: VAN DE SANDE, Jac. Z., Boekverkooper
op de Groote Markt, in den Staten Bybel. 1766.

61 – Title page of *Tydkorting*, Vol. 1, Middelburg, 1766.

Acknowledgments

For this book, use was made of the logbook of Cornelis Eyks, published in 1766 under the title: *Noodlottige Gevallen van het Volk van het Schip* Amstelveen, *na deszelfs Verongelukken in dato 5 August 1763, op de Tocht van Batavia na Persiën, op hun weg door Arabiën overgekomen.*[88] The logbook was published by J. van der Sande of Middelburg, in a collection of monthly instalments entitled *Tydkorting* or *Magazyn der Heeren.*[89] The text covers 53 pages and is also referred to in this collection as the *Aantekeningen van Cornelis Eyks.*[90] The title page of the collection is shown on the facing page.

Furthermore, various documents from the voc archives in the Dutch National Archives, The Hague, were consulted and quoted along with their inventory numbers, as well as sources such as historical atlases and the website http://vocopvarenden.nationaalarchief.nl/.

The Zeeuws Archives in Middelburg were primarily consulted using the website http://www.zeeuwengezocht.nl.

For general nautical information, specialist encyclopedias were consulted, namely the *Maritieme geschiedenis der Nederlanden* (*Vol. 3*),[91] the *Maritieme Encyclopedie* by J. van Beylen et al., the *Encyclopedie van de Zeilvaart* and the *Zeilvaart Lexicon (Maritiem woordenboek)* by J. van Beylen, all published by De Boer Maritiem.

Use was made of the modern nautical chart BA 3785, Arabia; Oman — South-East Coast, *Port Salalah to Masirah*, British Admiralty, 2001.

For landscape analysis Google Earth proved to be very helpful.

---

88 The Fate of the People of the Ship Amstelveen, after the said Ship was wrecked on 5 August 1763 on the Voyage from Batavia to Persia, as befell them on their way through Arabia.
89 Pastime or Gentlemen's Magazine.
90 Notes of Cornelis Eyks.
91 The Naval History of the Netherlands (Vol. 3); Naval Encyclopedia; The Sailing Encyclopedia; The Sailing Lexicon (Naval Dictionary).

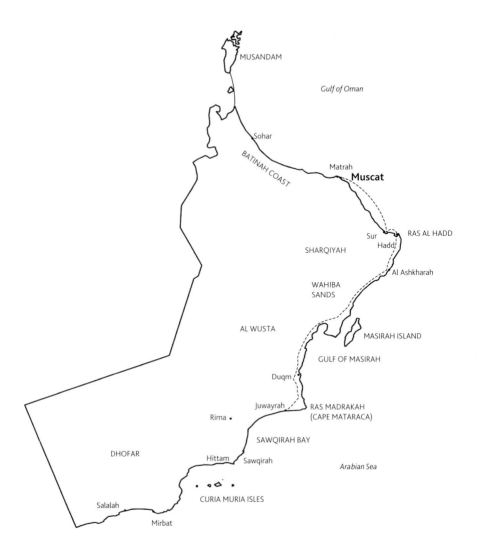

62 – The trek of the survivors from the beach of Ras Madrakah through the desert and along the coasts of Al Wusta and Sharqiyah to Hadd. Most of them sailed from there to Matrah or Muscat.

Finally: the fate of the Amstelveen has never been established for certain. It is only known where one might search for the remains of the wreck and remnants from the ship with a chance of success. The ship was stranded near Juwayrah, close to the coast (see p. 132), probably at high tide and with a heightened water level due to the monsoon. In the autumn, with an offshore wind and at low tide, the remains of the wreck would have lain almost dry, close to a magnificent beach.

Bibliography

Abbas bin Ghulam Rasool al-Zadjali, *Pictures of Oman*. Ruwi, 1979.

Barend-van Haeften, M.L., *Op reis met de VOC. De openhartige dagboeken van de zusters Lammens en Swellengrebel*. Zutphen, 1996.

Barend-van Haeften, M.L., *Oost-Indië gespiegeld. Nicolaas de Graaff, een schrijvend chirurgijn in dienst van de VOC*. Zutphen, 1992.

Beguin Billecocq, Xavier, *Oman. Vingt-cinq Siècles de Récits de Voyage/Twenty-five Centuries of Travel Writing*. Paris, 1994.

Bonke, H., *De zeven reizen van de Jonge Lieve. De biografie van een VOC-schip, 1760–1781*. Nijmegen, 1999.

Bundy, G., R.J. Connor & C.J.O. Harrison, *Birds of the Eastern Province of Saudi Arabia*. London, 1989.

Chaudhuri, K.N., *Trade and Civilisation in the Indian Ocean. An Economic History from the Rise of Islam to 1750*. Cambridge, 1985.

Fahad al-Said (pref.), *Oman, a seafaring nation*. Ministry of Information and Culture, Muscat, 1978.

Gaastra, Femme S., *De geschiedenis van de VOC*. Zutphen, 2002.

Gallagher, M. & M.W. Woodcock, *The Birds of Oman*. London, 1980.

Gawronski, Jerzy, *De Equipagie van de Hollandia en de Amsterdam. VOC-bedrijvigheid in 18de-eeuws Amsterdam*. Amsterdam, 1996.

Gelder, R. v. & R. Kistemaker, *Amsterdam, The Golden age 1275–1795*. New York, 1983.

Groenewegen, G., *Verzameling van Vier en tachtig Stuks Hollandse Schepen*. Rotterdam 1789 (Reprint 1967).

Groesbeek, J.W., *Amstelveen — acht eeuwen geschiedenis*. Amsterdam, 1966.

Hamilton, A., *An Arabian Utopia: the Western Discovery of Oman*. London, 2010.

Hawley, D., *Oman and its Renaissance*. London, 1987.

Historische Beschryving der Reizen. Published by the Wed. S. Schouten en Zoon, J. Hayman, J. Roman a.o., Vol. 16, 1757.

Hoek, C.W., *Shifting Sands. Social-economic development in al-Sharqiyah region, Oman*. Diss. KU Nijmegen, 1998.

Howarth, D., *Dhows*. London, 1977.

Huis, F., *Martelgang naar Muscat*. De Telegraaf, 13 Febr. 1993.

Jacobs, E.M., *Koopman in Azië. De handel van de Verenigde Oost-Indische Compagnie tijdens de 18de eeuw*. Zutphen, 2000.

Jong, O. de, *Schipbreuk in Bengalen. Avonturen van een V.O.C.-matroos.* Emmen, 2006.

Jörg, C.J.A., *The Geldermalsen. History and Porcelain.* Groningen, 1986.

Kooreman, M., *The Quest of the Amstelveen.* PDO News 4/94 & 1/95.

Kuipers, J.J.B. & J. Francke, *Geschiedenis van Zeeland. De canon van ons Zeeuws verleden.* Zutphen, 2009.

Lindeman, G.J., *De VOC-schepen Amstelland en Amstelveen.* Amstel Mare, 19, 1, 2008.

Leuftink, A.E., *Harde heelmeesters. Zeelieden en hun dokters in de 18de eeuw.* Zutphen, 2008.

Marsden, P., *The Wreck of the Amsterdam.* Hutchinson, London, 1974.

Ministry of Information, *Oman 2009–2010.* Muscat, 2009.

Mols, L. & B. Boelens (ed.). *Oman.* Amsterdam, 2009.

Niebuhr, C., *Reize naar Arabië en andere omliggende landen.* Amsterdam/ Utrecht, 2 vol., 1776–1780.

Oman, a Seafaring Nation. Ministry of Information and Culture, the Sultanate of Oman. Muscat, 1979.

Paesie, R., *Het VOC-schip Ravesteyn. De laatste reis van een Zeeuwse Oostin- diëvaarder.* Amsterdam, 1999.

Parmentier, J. (red.), *Uitgevaren voor de kamer Zeeland.* Zutphen, 2006.

Philippa, M., *Koffie, kaffer en katoen. Arabische woorden in het Nederlands.* Amsterdam, 1989.

Randier, J., *Marine Navigation Instruments.* London, 1980.

Roeper, V.D. & G.J.D. Wildeman, *Reizen op papier. Journalen en reisverslagen van Nederlandse ontdekkingsreizigers, kooplieden en avonturiers.* Zutphen, 1996.

Roeper, V. & R. van Gelder, *In dienst van de Compagnie. Leven bij de VOC in honderd getuigenissen (1602–1799).* Amsterdam, 2002.

Roos, D. *Zeeuwen en de VOC,* Middelburg, 1987.

Salmon, Th., *Hedendaagsche Historie of Tegenwoordige Staat van Alle Volkeren.* Vol. IV. Isaak Tirion, Amsterdam, 1732.

Saunders, D., *A Journal of the Travels and Sufferings of Daniel Saunders.* Salem (Mass., USA), 1794. Gale ECCO print, 2011.

Schilder, G. & H. Kok, *Sailing for the East. History & Catalogue of Manuscript Charts on vellum VOC 1602–1799.* Houten, 2010.

Schweiger-Lerchenfeld, A. von, *Het Oosten.* Rotterdam, 1884.

Serjeant, R.B., *Early Islamic and mediaeval trade and commerce in the Yemen.* In: Werner Daum (ed.), *Yemen, 3000 Years of Art and Civilisation in Arabia Felix.* Innsbruck, Frankfurt/M., Amsterdam, 1987.

Sigmond, J.P., *Nederlandse zeehavens tussen 1500 en 1800.* Amsterdam, 1989.

Slot, B.J., *Nederlanders aan de kusten van Oman.* The Hague, 1991.

Slot, B.J., *The Origins of Kuwait.* Leiden, New York, 1991.

Slot, B.J., *Voc-schip in Oman: de Amstelveen*. Oman-Magazine 1, 2, The Hague/ Bruxelles, 1993.

Walsmit, E., H. Kloosterboer, N. Persoon en R. Ostermann, *Spiegel van de Zuiderzee. Geschiedenis en Cartobibliografie van de Zuiderzee en het Hollands Waddengebied*. Houten, 2009.

Zandvliet, K., *Mapping for Money*. Amsterdam, 2002.